T0246427

MARKED MAN

MARKED MAN

FRANK SERPICO'S
INSIDE BATTLE AGAINST
POLICE CORRUPTION

JOHN FLORIO AND OUISIE SHAPIRO

Roaring Brook Press
New York

Published by Roaring Brook Press
Roaring Brook Press is a division of Holtzbrinck Publishing
Holdings Limited Partnership
120 Broadway, New York, NY 10271 • fiercereads.com

Library of Congress Control Number 2023024514

Our books may be purchased in bulk for promotional, educational,
or business use. Please contact your local bookseller or the Macmillan
Corporate and Premium Sales Department at (800) 221–7945 ext. 5442
or by email at MacmillanSpecialMarkets@macmillan.com.

First edition, 2024
Book design by Ellen Duda
Printed in the United States of America

ISBN 978-1-250-62195-5
1 3 5 7 9 10 8 6 4 2

For NYPD Captain William Florio,
an honest cop
—J. F.

To those brave souls who speak up
in the face of wrongdoing
—O. S.

CONTENTS

A Note to the Reader

We have tried to be as accurate as possible in telling the story of Frank Serpico's battle against corruption in the New York City Police Department.

To reconstruct the scenes in this book, we relied on our interviews with Serpico, along with his many published essays and articles. We also turned to historical accounts, including Peter Maas's book *Serpico* and newspaper accounts of the day. For dialogue, we relied on the same sources. When there was no official record, we have used our own words to create dialogue that captures the essence of what the speakers intended.

In all cases, we have presented what we believe to be a truthful depiction of these events.

One final note: Throughout the book, most of which takes place during the 1960s, we refer to members of the NYPD as policemen, patrolmen, and plainclothesmen in keeping with the language of the time. Women were not fully integrated into the department until the 1970s. Only then did all members of the force become known as police officers.

MARKED
MAN

Preface

778 Driggs Avenue, Williamsburg, Brooklyn, 1971

THE ACTION'S GOING DOWN IN 3G. MAMBO, THE GUY INSIDE, is moving heroin.

Three plainclothes cops hatch a plan. The bearded one can speak Spanish. He'll knock on the door, act like a junkie, say he's looking to make a buy. When the door opens, they'll grab Mambo with the stash in his hand. They'll cuff him, drag him to the precinct. Nice and clean.

The bearded cop knocks. He's got his .38 snub-nose by his side, his face pressed against the peephole. The other two wait—one on the landing, the other three feet away.

Mambo opens the door. Too slowly. The cop rams his shoulder into it, breaks the security chain, tries to push his way in. Mambo pushes back. It's a standoff—the cop is stuck, one leg inside the apartment, the other out.

The cop raises his gun, points it toward Mambo. Then he shouts for his partners, turns his head, looks for them. Bad move.

When he turns back around, he's hit by a burst of light and the blast of a handgun.

– Welcome –

My name is Frank Serpico. I'm eighty-seven, and I've been carrying that bullet in my head for more than fifty years. I'm deaf in one ear, and I walk with a limp.

To you, my story may sound like ancient history, but it wasn't always that way. In 1973, Al Pacino played me in a movie called *Serpico*. The film was a big hit— the American Film Institute ranks the character of Serpico on its list of all-time movie heroes. The minute that film hit the theaters, my name became the stuff of legend.

Everybody, it seemed, knew the name of the cop who bucked the system.

The Hollywood hoopla has since died down, of course, but I'm still persona non grata in the NYPD. And, believe it or not, I still get hate mail from active and retired officers.

Police make up a peculiar subculture in society. More often than not, they have their own moral code, an "us against them" attitude. And it's enforced by a blue wall of silence, which can be even stronger than the omertà, the code of silence in the Mafia. You know the basics: Open your mouth, and you're no longer one of us; you're one of them.

I opened my mouth. I'm one of them.

In 1972, I was given the Medal of Honor, the NYPD's highest award for bravery in action, but it wasn't for what you would think. It wasn't for taking on an army of corrupt cops; it was for getting shot in the line of duty. They handed me the medal like they were tossing me a pack of cigarettes.

An ex-con once told me that a precinct captain said, "If it wasn't for that fuckin' Serpico, I could've been a millionaire today." The ex-con went on to say, "Frank, you don't seem to understand; they had a well-oiled moneymaking machine going, and you came along and threw a handful of sand in the gears."

That's how it was—the entire New York City Police Department was out to get me. Even now, it strikes me as odd that some people see me as an enemy of law enforcement, that I'm not welcome by police in my own city. Because as far back as I can remember, all I wanted to be was a member of the NYPD.

All I wanted to be was one of New York's finest.

Chapter One

WHEN FRANK WAS A KID, HIS NIGHTTIME RITUAL INVOLVED turning on his bedside radio at nine o'clock sharp to listen to his favorite show. "And now," the announcer would intone, the room pitch-black except for the glow coming from the radio dial, "another thrilling episode of *Gang Busters!*"

The show branded itself "the only national program that brings you authentic police case histories." The stories were thrilling. "The Broadway Bandits." "The Alcatraz Prison Riot." "The Death Mask Killer." For Frank, tuning in was like going to detective school. Even better, the episodes came complete with squealing tires, wailing sirens, popping gunshots, and satisfying endings—because every week the good guys won.

Those were the days of Fiorello La Guardia. Elected New York City mayor during the Great Depression, in 1934, La Guardia was a determined reformer. It was easy to admire him; he was a five-foot-tall dynamo. Everything he did, he did with fervor. And he refused to abide by the dictates of the Republican Party, which had helped get him elected. He got rid of the old-time, double-dealing politicians and their bosses who were running the city. He reorganized city government, unified the subway system, created public housing for the poor, and built playgrounds and public parks across the city. He cracked down on the mobsters who were running illegal gambling outfits, and he launched a public crusade to clean up a corrupt police force.

During a newspaper strike that affected thirteen million readers, La Guardia went on the radio and read comic strips out loud to the children of the city. He chose *Dick Tracy*, about the popular police detective who battled gangsters, bank robbers, and crooked politicians. When the mayor finished reading, he said to his listeners, "Say, children, what does it all mean? It means that dirty money never brings any luck . . . No, dirty money always brings sorrow and sadness and misery and disgrace."

Born two years after La Guardia's election, Francesco Serpico was raised by his parents, Vincenzo and Maria, who had met in Italy and come to America shortly after getting married. Young Francesco, called Frank, played marbles, hide-and-seek, and stickball on the streets of Brooklyn, New York. His neighborhood, Bedford-Stuyvesant, was a melting pot of immigrants from Italy and Eastern Europe, as well as Black Americans, all of whom struggled to earn respect in a city that could be cold, uncaring, and cruel.

Mayor Fiorello La Guardia addresses New York City in a radio broadcast.

Brooklyn, circa 1947

One story has young Frank working in his father's cobbler shop after school. His jobs were menial—dragging a magnetic shoe horn across the floor to gather the nails that had fallen from the cobbler's benches—but he loved watching his father at work. A master of his trade, Vincenzo had apprenticed to a shoemaker in Italy at the age of nine and still repaired every shoe by hand with painstaking precision. Standing by his bench, gripping a row of nails between his lips, he would pick up a shoe with a broken heel and lay it face down on the bench. Then with one hand he'd pull a nail from his mouth and with his other hand grab his hammer. *Wham! Wham! Wham!* In went the nails, a bull's-eye every time. Frank admired his father's work ethic. By spending endless hours in that shop—on many nights he never made it home at all—Vincenzo had earned enough money to buy a house in which he and Maria could raise their four children: Pasquale, Tina, Salvatore, and Frank.

One day, when working at the shop, Frank buffed the oxfords of a uniformed police officer. Frank was as proud as could be—he was shining the shoes of the law! He polished the leather until it looked like new, then watched, stunned, as the cop stood up and walked out the door without paying. Frank never forgot the guy's arrogance. Nor did he forget the cop coming back a week later for another shine.

"Ten cents," Vincenzo said, holding out his hand. "Up front."

The cop grunted, left, and never returned.

Another time, an inspector from the labor department came by the shop and asked Vincenzo for Frank's working papers.

"What papers?" Vincenzo asked. "He's my son."

"It doesn't matter," the man said. "He's underage; he needs working papers."

Vincenzo's eyes narrowed. "You want my boy out in the street with the other bums? My boy will stay here where I can keep my eye on him. Here I teach him a trade."

With that, Vincenzo picked up a hammer and ordered the man out of the shop.

Throughout his life, Frank carried these memories of his father with him. Vincenzo might not have been a powerful man, but he had his own sense of morality, and it was an honorable one.

When Frank was thirteen, fate stepped in again, this time reinforcing his romantic vision of police work. His mother took him to visit his grandfather in Italy, where Frank met his uncle Nicolo. Nicolo was a member of the carabinieri, the specialized Italian military police who investigate Mafia groups and other criminal enterprises. Their uniforms alone commanded respect: double-breasted, brass-buttoned jackets and pants with a bold red stripe running along the outside of the leg. Italians took notice. They looked up to them.

Nicolo had the swagger of somebody important, the air of a man with confidence. Why wouldn't he? He was respected. He carried a Beretta rifle. He was *somebody*. He was, in the eyes of young Frank, an honest-to-goodness crime fighter.

By the time he was in high school, Frank found ways to play the part of a policeman, including making his own zip gun out of rubber bands and a car antenna. When working properly, the gun could discharge a .22-caliber bullet forcefully enough to hurt somebody standing a few feet away. Unfortunately, Frank was better at *making* zip guns than using them—he wound up in the hospital one day after shooting himself in the arm.

As he sat wearing a fresh bandage, two policemen came by to ask him some questions.

"Where's the gun?" they said.

"I don't have a gun," Frank told them. "I found a bullet, took off its tip, and it exploded."

The officers looked at each other. The story was obviously a lie.

"Where do you go to school?" one of them said.

"St. Francis Prep. And I want to be a cop, just like you guys."

"Well," the other said, "if you don't smarten up, you'll never make it that far."

They let Frank go with a warning, but he got the message, loud and clear. From that point forward, he would play by the rules.

FRANCIS VINCENT SERPICO
JANUARY 1954
St. Teresa's
Intramurals 1, 2, 3, 4; Science Club 1; Cafeteria 3; Band 1, 2, 3, 4; Orchestra 1, 2, 3, 4.

Frank graduates St. Francis Prep, 1954.

So after high school Frank joined the army, spending two years as an infantryman in South Korea. But he was still angling to jump on to the police force. When he came home, he took a job as a part-time security guard and studied police science at night. He went so far as to show up for class in navy-blue trousers and a tan trench coat, just like the cops on the TV show *Dragnet*.

In 1956, when Frank turned twenty, he was eligible to take the entrance exam at the New York City Police Academy—and that's just what he did. While waiting for his appointment to come through, he went to work for the Youth Board, a division of the Mayor's Office, helping calm tensions among juvenile gangs.

In 1959, he was finally accepted into the academy and found himself standing in front of the old red-brick building in lower Manhattan. At the entrance, a sign greeted him and all police cadets: "A clear conscience is the softest pillow." Frank took courses in ethics, police conduct, investigation, arrest, and the handling of prisoners. He trained in the use of firearms and was tested on physical strength and agility. He learned how to deliver a baby in the event that an ambulance was delayed. He took a crash course in municipal and criminal law. And he attended lectures on psychology, race relations, civil defense, city government, and juvenile delinquency.

One instructor advised, "If you catch a kid stealing, don't call him a little thief. Ask him where he got the stuff."

Another posed a question: "Three suspicious men are found in a hallway. If one of them drops something on the floor, what's the first thing you do?"

A rookie shot up his hand. "Frisk 'em."

"Well, no," the instructor said. "If there's more than one patrolman, separate the suspects. If you're the only one present, tell them not to talk with each other. That way they can't make up a story between them."

Instructors at the academy emphasized that police officers were cast in the role of "protector of life and property of every citizen. You will risk your life in the service of people whose names you don't even know."

Frank gave the instructors his full attention. These were the kinds of guys who could teach him how to be a good cop, maybe even a better person. This was the place to be to broaden your mind; the academy was teaching the importance of the law—and how to help people.

But one veteran officer pulled Frank aside to share his own take. "Listen to me," he said. "Don't go crazy. Nobody likes a cowboy. Just clock in and clock out, you'll be fine."

Frank knew this kind of cop, too. He'd seen plenty of these do-nothing guys growing up in Brooklyn—like the patrolman who'd come by his father's shop for a free shoeshine. That wasn't the kind of cop Frank wanted to be.

"Thanks for the advice," Frank said, itching to start the job and follow his own instincts.

In April 1960, along with nearly three hundred other recruits, he graduated from the academy and officially became a New York City policeman.

At the swearing-in ceremony, held at City College's Baruch School of Business and Public Administration, Police Commissioner Stephen Kennedy made a point of telling the class to crack down on gambling operations. The enforcement of gambling laws was a "farce," he said, because so many violators were paying fines instead of receiving jail time.

This was no surprise to Frank. Any kid growing up in Brooklyn knew gambling bosses were roaming the streets, seemingly free of repercussions. And those same guys were involved in bigger operations that brought drugs and guns into the local neighborhoods.

Rookie officer Frank Serpico

New York's War on Gambling

Police Commissioner Stephen Kennedy, 1961

For centuries, New York politicians had railed against gambling as immoral, claiming it tempted poor and otherwise honest citizens into risking what little money they had. In their eyes, gambling was evil; professional criminals used it as a springboard to gain a foothold in more nefarious operations, such as narcotics and prostitution.

Police Commissioner Stephen Kennedy, who held the position from 1955 to 1961, took a similar stance. He declared war on gambling and directed the NYPD to enforce the laws against it. Under his watch, police precincts across the city had bulletin boards covered in photos of known gambling bosses. Each picture showed the boss's name, address, place of operation, type of gambling, and date of last arrest.

Like every commissioner before him, Kennedy recognized the temptations that came with carrying a badge. He warned his officers to stay clean and maintain their integrity. He refused to stand for the idea that there would always be a few rotten apples on the force. "Rotten apples," he said, "had better be taken out before the whole barrel spoils. Inefficiency, ineptitude and corruption must be rooted out."

After the ceremony, a beaming Vincenzo hugged his son.

"I'm proud of you," he said to Frank. "Policemen help people."

As a rookie cop, Frank was still living at home with his parents—but the face of his neighborhood had changed. Bedford-Stuyvesant had become densely populated, predominantly African American, and one of the poorest neighborhoods in the city. Frank left for the 81st Precinct on nearby Ralph Avenue and took on his first assignment: Walk his beat. Stop crime. Be a cop.

He donned his uniform, ready to protect local citizens from muggers, criminals, and drug pushers. Then he patrolled his six-block turf, armed with a badge, a gun, and the life lessons he'd learned at the cobbler shop.

Frank knew he was no run-of-the-mill cop.

While most police officers had buzz cuts, Frank grew his hair into a stylish pompadour. While many were beefy, Frank stood only five-foot-eight and had a slender frame. He loved opera and jazz, read philosophy, and even wrote poetry.

For most cops, policing was a steady paycheck. Carrying a nightstick was easier than a lot of other jobs, like working construction or pushing racks of clothing through the streets of Manhattan's garment district. But Frank noticed that few of his fellow recruits cared about justice. And not one of them had any aspirations to become a detective and investigate important cases.

Frank was still a raw recruit at the Eight-One—cop talk for the 81st Precinct—when a fellow patrolman suggested they eat lunch at the local deli.

"Good food?" Frank asked.

"Nah, they're on the arm."

"What do you mean?" Frank said. "I don't have to pay the guy?"

"Well, you know, leave him a quarter or something."

Frank didn't want a free meal. He earned a salary, could pay for his own food, and never bought things he couldn't afford. No house. No boat. No fancy wristwatch. Who needed that stuff?

It wasn't long after the deli conversation that Frank found himself in the squad car with his new partner, driving through the streets of the Eight-One. When they saw a car blow through a red light, they sped up to it and motioned for the driver to pull over. The guy did as he was told, and Frank got out of the squad car to walk over to him.

"Can't we take care of this now?" the driver said, reaching into his pocket and pulling out his wallet.

"You're not trying to pay me off, are you?"

Frank was ready to charge the guy with running the red light and attempting to bribe an officer, but his partner came over and told Frank to go back to the squad car.

His partner spoke with the driver, and when he returned to the car, he was holding thirty-five bucks, and thrust half of it toward Frank.

"Here you go," he said. "Your share."

"No," Frank said, waving him off. "I don't need that guy's money."

"You sure? Around here, we split everything down the middle."

"Yeah, I'm sure. But thanks anyway."

Frank went home that night wondering if this was the way all cops operated. Taking money? Using their power to get free meals? If this was police work, he didn't want any part of it.

Soon, and to his disappointment, Frank discovered that many of his fellow cops, especially those on overnight shifts, were sleeping on the job. The guys called it "cooping," but it didn't matter what name they gave it, they were shirking their responsibilities. Some slept in their patrol cars under the Brooklyn Bridge, some off the FDR Drive. Some set up their coops—that is, their sleep nooks—in schools and firehouses. One coop, located in a park in Brooklyn, was so well known in the neighborhood that residents called it the "annex." Frank didn't get it. What was the matter with these guys?

Why didn't they do what he did? Just walk your beat and do your job. If it's too cold, throw on a pair of thermal underwear. You're not going to catch any burglars if you're asleep under a blanket.

Instead of getting angry, Frank doubled down on his original plan. He'd work hard, protect the public, and with a little luck, become a detective. Those guys weren't lazy. They had brains—it took smarts to gather information, sift through evidence, track down suspects, and build cases. But Frank knew the days of becoming a detective by performing an act of bravery were over. Since he didn't have any friends in high places, his only path to detective was through the plainclothes division. Those cops were a step up from uniform patrol. And they got special training, too. They knew how to track down drug dealers, prostitutes, and gambling bosses—and if you were good, you'd get picked for the detective squad.

It was a plum assignment, and Frank went for it.

One day, during his rookie year, he had just finished handling traffic at a school crossing when a young man raced up to him and grabbed his elbow.

"Officer," the Black man said between gasps of air. "Come quick! My wife is having a baby."

Frank raced through the streets, following the young man, who led him to an old tenement. Together, they vaulted up the stairs to a cramped, two-room apartment. In the bedroom, a young woman—she couldn't have been a day over twenty—was under a blanket, screaming.

"It's our first," the man told Frank. "I don't know what to do!"

"Call an ambulance," Frank said. "Now!"

"We don't have a phone."

"Then go next door and call from there. Hurry!"

Frank tossed his coat on the back of a chair, then went to the bathroom to wash his hands. He returned to the bedroom and, in his mind, ran through what he'd been taught at the academy.

Positioning himself between the woman's legs, he could see that the baby's head was already emerging. The ambulance was probably still minutes away, so he cupped his hands under the infant's head to support it. But there was a problem. The umbilical cord was wrapped around the baby's neck. As the woman pushed on instinct, the cord became tighter and tighter.

Frank had trained for this. Staying calm, he repeatedly tried slipping his finger under the cord to guide it over the baby's head. At last, he was able to free the cord and slide the baby out unharmed.

After the delivery, Frank turned the baby upside down, cleared out its mouth with his finger, and slapped its butt softly. The baby let loose a vigorous cry.

"Well, what do you know," he said to the mother over her baby's wails. "It's a boy."

When Frank turned around, the father was still in the doorway.

"What are you doing here? Didn't you call an ambulance?"

"No," the man said. "I was too scared to move."

Frank had a dilemma: At the academy, he'd been told to wait for the medical crew to cut the umbilical cord. But now, realizing he was on his own—and there was no time to go out to the street and look for a call box—he'd have to cut the cord himself.

"Boil some water," he told the father. "And we'll need some string. And a pair of scissors."

He rested the tender, brown-skinned baby on the mother's belly and tied a section of the sterilized string around the cord, a couple of inches from the baby's navel. Then he snipped the cord and wrapped a towel around the newborn.

When Frank left the apartment, he was as exhilarated as he was exhausted.

A week later, when Frank was walking his beat, the baby's father ran over to him.

"There you are!" the man said. "I've been looking for you. What's your name?"

"Serpico."

"No, I mean your first name."

"Frank. Frank Serpico."

The man looked at him and smiled. "That's what we're naming our son. We're calling him Frank. After you."

Frank smiled and shook the man's hand.

This was his city. And he was proud to patrol it.

In 1962, after two years at the Eight-One, Frank passed a test to work at the Bureau of Criminal Identification, an annex in lower Manhattan that housed criminal records used in city and federal investigations. Most cops saw the BCI as the first rung on the ladder to becoming a plainclothesman, and Frank was no different. He was happy to get the assignment, certain it would lead to becoming detective. He spent his days holed up in the office, processing fingerprint cards and sending them to the FBI to see if any local suspects had records outside of New York State. At night, he attended the City University of New York, working toward a bachelor's degree in police science.

Although the job was uneventful, Frank loved the electric atmosphere of downtown Manhattan. The BCI offices were close to Greenwich Village, a swath of narrow, crooked streets, five-story walk-ups, mom-and-pop restaurants, bookstores, and coffee shops where poets, artists, and college students gathered. Frank hung out at the local clubs—the Bitter End, the Village Vanguard, and Café Wha?—and he dated waitresses, actresses, singers, and dancers. Soon, he rented a tiny garden apartment that he would fill with records, books, artifacts from trips abroad, a lava lamp, two dogs, and a couple of goldfish bowls. He grew his hair, sprouted a full, dark beard, and took to wearing jeans and sandals.

To his friends in the Village, he was Paco, the nickname he'd

Greenwich Village's Café Wha? in the mid-sixties

picked up during his travels to Puerto Rico. To his fellow police officers, he was a beatnik, and beatniks were usually targeted, not embraced, by cops. But Frank liked being different; he saw no reason to dress like the other guys, especially when he was off duty.

The BCI inspector didn't agree.

He saw Frank as an outcast and reassigned him to uniformed foot patrol in the 70th Precinct in Brooklyn. Kicked out of the BCI, Frank was back to walking a beat in a button-down patrolman's uniform.

But the 70th Precinct captain, Joseph Fink, sensed an opportunity in Frank's off-duty getups and occasionally put him on plainclothes patrol anyway. For Frank, the assignment was a dream. It did more than get him back on track to becoming detective; it also allowed him to keep watch over the neighborhood.

One afternoon, as Frank parked his car before reporting to duty, he spotted smoke coming from a three-story building across the street. He grabbed his flashlight, ran to the apartment house, and entered the ground-floor apartment. One wall of the kitchen was engulfed in flames, and somewhere in the apartment a baby was crying.

Following the sounds of the cries down the hall, Frank discovered, in a small cubicle, a baby in a crib. He scooped up the infant and held it to his chest. Racing through the apartment, he found, in another room, a man lying on his back, stretched across a bed.

He poked the man, hoping he hadn't passed out from smoke inhalation.

"Wake up," Frank said, pushing even harder.

"Huh?" the man said, stirring.

"Get up! Now! The place is on fire. Let's go."

The man jumped out of bed, his face a mix of fear and panic, and nodded toward the baby. "Thank God you're here," he said to Frank. Then, his eyes still wide, he grabbed Frank's arm. "My dogs are in the basement. I've got to get 'em."

Frank gave the man his flashlight and carried the baby outside, where a crowd was watching the flames engulf the building. Frank handed the infant to one of the neighbors and ran back inside, this time heading upstairs to the second-floor apartment. But racing up that flight was a mistake. The action forced him to take bigger gulps of black, sooty air. When he reached the landing, he could barely make his way through the smoke to find the apartment.

He kicked in the door, and flames shot at him like dragons' tongues. He couldn't go inside; the fire was too powerful, and the smoke too thick. He turned and ran back down the stairs, leaving the building to clear his lungs. Outside, people were pointing toward a third-story window where a woman was holding two children and shouting for help.

The upper portion of the building was set back, trimmed by a ledge that was wide enough for a grown man to walk. Frank shimmied up the drainpipe, a neighbor trailing close behind. They crawled along the ledge until they were underneath the woman in the window. Extending his arms up, Frank told her to hand him the children. With the man securing him, Frank took each child, one at a time, and passed them to the onlookers below.

In the distance, sirens screamed.

"Hang on!" Frank shouted up to the woman. "The fire department's almost here."

"I can't stay in here," she said. "I'm coming, too."

"No, no, we won't be able catch you," Frank said.

"I'm coming, too!"

Frank tried to stop her, but she was already climbing out of the window. Seeing no alternative, he locked arms with the other man.

"Okay, jump!" Frank yelled.

The woman did just that—and hit the target—but she plowed right through their grip and tumbled onto the ledge. By then, firemen had arrived with a ladder and helped her down to the ground. She walked away from the incident with no injuries other than a bump on her head and a pair of bruised knees.

When Frank reached the ground, he got an equally pleasant surprise: The second-floor apartment, the one he couldn't enter, turned out to be empty.

In anybody's book, Frank was a hero. But when he got back to the police station, nobody seemed to care.

"Put on your damned uniform," said a precinct lieutenant, a guy named Ferrara. "You have to direct traffic."

Frank did as he was told, but in the middle of his post, he started feeling sick. He phoned into the precinct from a call box.

"I don't feel very good," he told Ferrara.

"Well," the lieutenant said. "You've got two choices. Suck it up and man your post, or take a sick day. There's no in-between."

Frank hated to take sick days, but he said he'd opt for some time off. Soon, a police car was driving him to the hospital. It turned out that he was suffering from smoke inhalation; the fumes inside that building were too much for a pair of human lungs. The doctors gave Frank oxygen and sent him home. After two weeks, he was back on the job.

But not a single boss, not Ferrara, not anybody, acknowledged his having saved five people from a burning building.

In 1966, Frank was reassigned to the plainclothes squad at Brooklyn's 90th Precinct. It turned out to be a good fit. The neighborhood was a hot spot for drugs and illegal gambling, and before long, he was arresting one drug dealer after another.

The Nine-O, 1965

But his most heroic act at the Nine-O had nothing to do with plainclothes work. In fact, he wasn't even on the clock the night it happened. He'd gone to the movies in Manhattan with his date, Shirley, and was taking her home to Brooklyn around midnight. They'd just driven over the Williamsburg Bridge and were idling on Frank's Honda motorcycle at a red light when gunshots—along with the unmistakable flashes that come from a pistol's muzzle— pierced the air a block ahead of them. From where he was sitting, Frank could make out three men leaning over a slumped figure on the sidewalk, their bodies silhouettes under the glow of a streetlamp.

"Quick, hide behind that pole," he told Shirley, nodding toward a steel pillar supporting the elevated train. "When the subway comes, take it home and I'll meet up with you later."

Shirley jumped off the bike, shouting, "Be careful!"

Frank rode slowly toward the scene, staying in the shadows, rolling his bike behind a small group of bystanders who were gawking at the three gunmen.

Two of the shooters took off on foot, running down the street, nearly impossible to tail. But the third guy climbed into a waiting gold Oldsmobile that drove off in the opposite direction.

Frank followed, staying far enough behind to avoid being noticed. Memorizing the license plate number—if he lost the car, he'd put out an APB—he trailed the Olds as it screeched around corners, cut down side streets, circled blocks, and doubled back to the area of the shooting. Finally, the car pulled to the curb, where the other two shooters were waiting, still breathing heavily from their two-legged escape.

Frank knew enough Spanish to understand what the suspects were saying as they scrambled into the car: "We need to get the hell out of here before the cops see us."

The Olds sped off, and Frank followed it again. He turned off his headlight and maintained his distance about a block behind, weaving around pedestrians and staying clear of parked cars. At one point, Frank's Honda skidded for a quarter block; he barely managed to keep it under his legs and the Olds in his crosshairs.

Finally, the car came to a stop next to an empty lot. The passenger door flew open and one of the gunmen got out, a pistol in each hand.

Frank hopped off his motorcycle, drew his service revolver, and, staying out of sight, scrambled to a parked sedan. He lay sprawled across the car's trunk—only feet from the gunman—and aimed his revolver at the guy's chest.

"Police," he said. "Drop the guns."

The guy spun around, ready to shoot, but he couldn't see where the voice was coming from. "La policía!" he shouted to his buddies, then ran back toward the Oldsmobile—but his friends took off without him.

Frank let the car go and stayed on the third gunman. He fired his revolver into the air as a warning shot, but the guy ran off, trying to leg his way to freedom. Giving chase across the lot, Frank caught up with him and tackled him to the ground. The two men landed with a bone-rattling thud and grappled on the pavement, but Frank managed to climb on top of the guy and lock his arm behind his back. He rummaged through the gunman's pockets and pulled out a loaded pistol.

Having disarmed his suspect, Frank kept his revolver extended as he inched slowly to a police box on a nearby lamppost to call for backup.

In minutes, two squad cars appeared; a couple of cops jumped out, threw the suspect into the back seat, and headed back to the Nine-O.

Frank learned afterward that he'd nabbed a man who was wanted for four previous felonies. The night Frank caught them, the three gunmen had gone too far when intimidating a neighborhood bar owner—that was the man Frank had seen lying on the ground—in an effort to muscle in on his and other local businesses.

Figuring he'd be rewarded for his bravery, Frank showed up for work the next day with his head held high. But all he got were hostile looks from his superiors, who wanted to know why Frank was chasing criminals in his off-hours. Why, the inspector asked, was he anywhere near the precinct when he wasn't on the clock? Was Frank's date married? Were they having an affair?

The questions seemed ridiculous, but Frank answered them one at a time. No, they weren't having an affair. No, he hadn't been looking for trouble. Yes, he really had stumbled upon a crime and felt it was his duty to help.

Finally, satisfied that Frank was on the level, the inspector put out his hand and shook Frank's.

"Good work," he said. "I'll put you in for a commendation."

Sure enough, Frank received an official citation for "alertness and intelligent police action." But now he understood what the veteran cop at the academy had meant when he said nobody likes a cowboy.

Frank continued doing his job, keeping his nose clean, arresting drug dealers, trying his best not to make waves. On a steamy 90-degree August day in 1966, he worked the riot detail of the 13th Division in Brooklyn. As he walked out of the parking garage underneath the 13th Division offices, a fellow cop approached him.

"Serpico, right?"

"Yeah, that's me."

"Here. I've been saving this for you," the cop said, holding out a white envelope, then tagging its source with an antisemitic slur. "It's from Jewish Max."

"Who's he?" Frank said, purposely keeping his hand at his side. "And what's in the envelope?"

"What the hell do I care? It yours."

The cop thrust it into Frank's hand and walked away.

Frank got in his car and took a closer look at the envelope. In the top left corner, a string of handwritten numbers—starting at 4,000 and working their way down—had been scratched out. Below the scratch marks was the number 300 in pencil.

Inside were three hundred-dollar bills.

He'd never heard of Jewish Max, but he knew one thing: The guy's money didn't belong to him.

And he didn't want it.

– A Word About the Police –

When I think back on those days, I remember a lot more than that envelope. I remember a police department that was totally broken.

You know the story about the burning building? The time I saved all those people? You probably think I got an official commendation, or had my picture on the cover of the *Daily News*, right? Instead, I got bupkes. Nobody ever said it, but I believe the department ignored me because the people I saved were Black.

Here's an example of how the police thought back then: One time, when I was a rookie cop, I was working with an older guy, and the two of us got called to an apartment where a woman was giving birth. When we got inside, a Black woman was lying on a bare mattress on the floor. Her two older kids were sitting nearby, anxiously waiting for the baby to come. Things went smoothly, and a boy was born without any complications.

When we walked out of the building, my partner, an old hairbag—that's cop talk for a burned-out officer—said to me, "That kid would've been better off if we just threw him in the garbage."

I knew he'd said it because the infant was Black. It sickened me. It was all I could do not to quit my job right then and there. I said to him, "How do you know he won't be another James Baldwin?"

And he said to me, "Who's that?"

That said it all. The guy was ignorant. He'd never even heard of James Baldwin, one of the great writers and thinkers of the twentieth century.

It was a lesson for me about man's inhumanity to man.

Of course, back then, I was just starting to find out all these things about my fellow men in blue—the racism, the laziness, and the corruption.

Which brings us back to the envelope.

Chapter Two

FRANK HELD THE CASH AND LOOKED AROUND THE GARAGE. A few cops were walking through the place, heading to their cars, but no one seemed to notice what had just happened. Or maybe they didn't care.

Was this $300 meant for him? For the squad?

People on the street spoke about bribing officers. John Lindsay, who'd been elected mayor in 1965, had built his campaign on cleaning up the force. The cops' reputation for being corrupt was well-earned, but was the system so out of whack that policemen were handing each other wads of money right out in the open, with their superiors working one flight up?

Frank slipped the envelope into his shirt pocket, drove back to the Nine-O, and hid it in the back of his locker.

It wasn't long before he found out why he'd been given the money. It was his share of a recent payoff. Jewish Max, a gambling boss no doubt, had paid off a cop in the Nine-O to let him skirt the law, and that cop had split the money with the boys. Most cops referred to this kind of cash as "the take" or "the pad," but a few wise guys called it "the nut" because cops were known to bury the cash in their backyards, the same way squirrels store their acorns through the winter. Whatever name you gave it, the money was dirty, plain and simple.

Mayor Lindsay on Crime

John Lindsay takes oath of office on December 31, 1965.

When John Lindsay took office in January 1966, he was determined to revamp a police force that he thought was "old and tired," and he vowed to make the city a "healthier, better, safer place to live."

Lindsay called for doubling the number of patrol cars to 3,200 and tripling the number of police motorcycles to 495, so residents would have "continuous mobile police surveillance in every block of the city."

It was a tall order.

Lindsay had taken the reins from Robert Wagner, who'd spent his twelve years as mayor battling crime. He'd beefed up the police force to twenty-eight thousand officers, two times that of an army infantry division. Still, by the end of his term, the city was averaging more than two murders a day.

Lindsay had also inherited a city torn by racial strife. In the eyes of many Black residents, the police didn't just offer insufficient protection; they also targeted Blacks more than they did white residents.

A major part of Lindsay's platform was to hold the police accountable for their actions. To that end, he reformed the existing review board, making it independent by adding four civilians to the three police officers already on the panel. The new board was multiracial and investigated complaints of police misconduct.

But the police union, the Patrolmen's Benevolent Association, pushed back, insisting that the cops could police themselves. The outraged union orchestrated a newspaper ad campaign showing a frightened young woman coming out of the subway alone on a dark street. The caption read, "The Civilian Review Board must be stopped. Her life . . . your life . . . may depend on it."

In less than a year, a citywide referendum abolished the review board—and a noncivilian unit, made up solely of police officials, took its place.

Nothing had changed.

Frank wasn't sure what to do. He didn't want any part of it. But he also knew his fellow cops wouldn't trust him if he didn't take the money. He didn't want to be an outcast. If he spoke up and told the boys to keep his share of the damned nut, he'd have the entire precinct out to get him. And that was a scary proposition.

He needed advice from somebody who wasn't taking money, somebody who was clean, who wasn't just another greasy cog in the dirty machine.

David Durk was a plainclothes cop he had met in the Criminal Investigation Course to become a plainclothesman. Frank remembered something Durk had said to him one day. When Frank had mentioned that Durk's collar was frayed, Durk said he'd worn it to show he had integrity. It was only a passing comment, but it didn't seem like something a dirty cop would say. And so, they'd hit it off.

Frank and Durk were both thirty-one, but that's where the similarities ended. At six feet, Durk stood four inches taller than Frank. The son of a physician, Durk had graduated from Amherst College and spent a year at Columbia Law School. He usually wore tailored gray flannel suits, the kind Ivy Leaguers dressed

David Durk

in, and he kept his prematurely graying hair neatly trimmed and combed. The biggest difference, though, was that Durk had connections, and he had made the most of them. He'd joined the force in 1963, four years after Frank, and had already moved up from foot patrolman in Harlem to staff detective in the Department of Investigation. The DOI, the special unit responsible for investigating city employees, reported directly to Mayor Lindsay.

Despite their differences, both men believed in public service. And both were adamantly opposed to cops taking bribes. In Durk's words, to be a cop was to "help an old lady walk the streets safely" and to allow "a storekeeper to make a living without keeping a shotgun under his cash register."

This was Frank's kind of guy.

Frank invited Durk to his apartment and told him the whole story, starting with the small payoffs and working his way up to the envelope from Jewish Max.

When Durk heard about the three hundred bucks, he leaned forward in his chair. "How structured is the system?"

Durk said he'd heard about the small stuff, a bar owner paying cops to let their customers double-park or a patrolman slipping cash to a roll-call officer in exchange for a cushy assignment. But this seemed as though the cops were running a business.

"Does your precinct captain know?" he asked Frank.

"I can't tell. But even if he does, I don't think he cares."

Durk nodded and walked over to the small bar by the window. "This could go all the way up the ladder," he said, pouring himself a splash of Scotch.

"No kidding," Frank said. "That's why I'm coming to you. You're in investigations—start investigating."

"Yeah, yeah, but the two of us can't take this on alone. We need somebody upstairs to get on board, somebody with some weight." Durk paced the room, swirling the whiskey in his glass. "I think we should bring this to my captain at the DOI."

"Are you talking about Foran?" Frank said. "I'm not sure I can trust that guy. Why not go right to the top? Let's go to Fraiman."

Durk shook his head. Arnold Fraiman was commissioner at the DOI—nobody there held a higher rank—but Durk clearly had reservations about meeting with him. "I don't know Fraiman well enough."

"Yeah, well, I don't know Foran at all."

"Jesus, Frank, the guy is legit. Foran's the most honest cop I know. What do you think? You're the only clean cop on the force?"

Frank didn't answer because his response would have been yes.

Durk gave Frank a snapshot of his relationship with Foran. They'd met taking night classes at Baruch College, and had spent hours sharing ideas about ways to fight police corruption. As it happened, Foran wound up running the squad of detectives at the DOI.

"I'll set up a meeting at the DOI tomorrow," Durk said, and downed the rest of his drink.

Then he reminded Frank to bring the envelope with him. That was the kind of hard evidence they'd need if they planned on accusing an entire police department of being on the take.

The DOI was located at 50 Pine Street in a dilapidated twelve-story building considered so unsafe that the city had ordered it vacated earlier that year. But the department continued running its operations out of there, and Captain Philip Foran's office was on the top floor.

With Durk by his side, Frank looked across the desk at Foran and told him everything he knew: the payoffs, the corruption, the pad, even the cooping.

As Foran leaned back in his chair, listening to Frank, he opened the envelope from Jewish Max and thumbed through the cash. "Why the hell would you take an envelope full of money from somebody you didn't know?"

Frank wasn't sure whether Foran expected a response, but he gave him one anyway.

"I told you, I didn't know what was in it. The guy handed it to me, so I took it. But the point isn't the envelope. It's that this kind of graft is going on throughout the precinct, and probably throughout the whole department."

Foran was all cop. He wore his uniform to code and seemed cocksure of himself. Resting both elbows on his desk, he took a hard look at Frank.

"You want to pursue this?" he said. "You'll need to bring it to Commissioner Fraiman. But if you do, the next thing you know, he'll have you sitting in front of a grand jury. Then word will get out that you're ratting out cops, and when it's all over, you'll be floating in the East River, face down."

Frank shot a glance at Durk before responding. "Captain, I'm only here because . . ."

"Or," Foran said, talking over Frank as he thrust his hand in the air, "you could shut your mouth and pretend the whole thing never happened."

Frank took a breath. "Okay, I guess I'll leave it alone," he said, figuring Foran was either dirty, lazy, or scared. "But what do I do with the money? I don't want it."

"That's up to you," Foran said, getting up and leading Frank and Durk to the door. "It's got nothing to do with me."

Frank left Foran's office as he'd entered it: holding $300 that he'd never wanted in the first place.

"I'm sorry, Frank," Durk said. "I had no idea Foran was a coward."

"I told you how hard it would be to get somebody to go along," Frank said. "If Foran's not in on it, then he knows somebody who is. I'm better off quitting. I can't keep doing this. I don't want to work in a place where I'm the only guy who's there to do his job."

"You've got a choice, you know," Durk said. "You can test the system. Go to your superiors and force the department to do something, or expose it for not doing anything. And if the guys at the top are dirty, you'll get them for a lot worse than turning a blind eye."

Frank thought about what Durk said. Most of all, though, he remembered the words his father had once told him at the cobbler shop: "Never run when you're right."

"Okay," Frank said. "Let's give it another shot."

A week later, Frank went to his sergeant at the Nine-O and said he needed to speak with him privately. He led the sarge to the plainclothes locker room, and once he made sure they were alone, opened his locker and took out the envelope.

"I don't want it," he said.

The sergeant nodded and said he understood. Then he took the envelope from Frank, pulled out the cash, and stuffed it into his own pocket.

It wasn't long before everyone in the station house knew about the money. Frank didn't hear the conversations, but based on the way he was being treated, it was easy enough to figure out what was being said: *Don't trust Frank; he's not one of us. Be careful and stay away from him.*

The situation only got worse when Frank began making arrests on his own. One day, he was working his shift, sitting in a bar, dressed in dirty jeans and a worn army jacket, staking out a gambling boss. As soon as the guy pulled a stack of betting slips from his pocket, Frank walked over, flashed his badge, and arrested him. But when he returned to the precinct to process the arrest, he got nothing but dirty stares from his fellow officers. He soon found out that the officers had already shaken the guy down—they'd taken their cut of his profits in exchange for leaving him alone.

It was clear to Frank, and apparently to every other cop at the Nine-O, that he was no longer welcome there. In their eyes, Frank was getting in the way of business. In Frank's eyes, these cops were hypocrites because they knew gambling didn't stop with a $10 bet on a football game. How could they pretend it wasn't so? That money would soon be back on the streets in the form of heroin. The chain was simple enough: Local gambling bosses sent the profits up the ladder. The guys at the top used the money to buy heroin, distribute it to kids on the street, and make a bundle in the process.

Frank tried to maneuver a transfer to the narcotics bureau in lower Manhattan. He showed up at the bureau in street clothes, hoping to impress the inspector with his disguise—long hair, jeans, and sandals—but he instantly got the sense he wasn't welcome there, either.

He soon found out he was right.

Narcotics rejected him, but not because he'd been the only clean cop at the Nine-O. Quite the opposite. From what Frank could tell, word was out that plainclothes cops working neighborhoods with a lot of gambling activity were on the take. So, despite Frank's spotless record, he carried with him the stink of his dirty colleagues.

The Harry Gross Scandal

Harry Gross leaves court after his arraignment, 1950.

In the early 1950s, a Brooklynite named Harry Gross nearly brought down the entire New York City Police Department. Gross had been running a $20-million-a-year illegal gambling operation, the largest in the city. His empire, which he ran out of a Brooklyn restaurant called the Dugout, extended across the city and into the suburbs. Stationed at a booth in the back of the restaurant, Gross dispatched an army of more than four hundred runners who took bets, answered phones, picked up money, and delivered payouts.

To keep from getting arrested, Gross paid the cops more than $1 million a year in bribe money he referred to as "ice." To Gross, the payments were simply a cost of doing business. He even paid "double ice" at Christmas and during boom times.

When the Brooklyn district attorney investigated him, Gross "flipped" and gave up the names of the cops on his payroll. There were more than a hundred names, ranging from plainclothesmen to the department's most senior officials. One of Gross's top aides testified in court that the payoffs were so large "it took two men to carry the bundles of money."

In the end, 22 police officers were convicted; another 240 either quit or were dismissed. The scandal also helped bring down Mayor William O'Dwyer and Police Commissioner William O'Brien, who both resigned. Gross received a reduced sentence in exchange for his testimony against the police and went to prison for eight years.

In the wake of the Harry Gross affair, the police department went on a public crusade, shutting down most gambling operations throughout the city. But the shutdowns didn't last long.

In December 1966, Frank was reassigned again, this time to the plainclothes unit of the 7th Division, a territory that included four precincts in the South Bronx. The unit's job was to enforce gambling laws in the seven-square-mile area, which was home to more than half a million residents. At one time the neighborhood had been solidly middle class, but it was now ravaged by poverty, drugs, and neglect. And, like so many other poor New York City neighborhoods, it was full of illegal gambling rackets.

Frank didn't know anybody there except for Robert Stanard, a plainclothesman who'd worked with Frank for a while at the Seven-O. But Frank and Stanard may as well have come from two different planets. Unlike Frank's scruffy hippie persona, Stanard had all the earmarks of a tough guy: a husky physique, a square jaw, and a habit of speaking out of one side of his mouth. Because of his horn-rimmed glasses, the guys at the Seven-O used to call him Clark Kent.

On January 2, 1967, Stanard asked Frank to accompany him on a civilian complaint.

"Sure," Frank said, throwing on a worn jacket that wouldn't arouse suspicion on the street.

They climbed into an unmarked car and drove to Otto's Bar and Grill, a local dive in the shadow of Yankee Stadium. The place was empty—it wasn't even noon—but it stank of stale whiskey and cigarettes.

Stanard walked up to the bar and ordered a couple of beers, one for him and one for Frank. Then he led Frank to a seat at the bar, a few stools away from the only other person in the place—a squat guy with thinning hair.

When the bartender walked away, Stanard nodded toward the guy on the stool. "That's Pasquale Trozzo."

Frank shot him a glance. Trozzo was positioned near a bank of pay phones, one of which rang every few minutes. He answered every time—the calls lasted only seconds—and each time he hung up, he scribbled something in his notebook. The guy had to be taking bets, most likely on the Rose Bowl and the Orange Bowl, the big college football games being played later that day.

Even more telling was the steady stream of men coming into the bar. Just like the phone calls, their conversations with Trozzo took less than a minute. They'd say hello and mumble a few words, which he'd jot down in his book. Sometimes they stayed for a drink, sometimes they left, but it didn't matter. There was no law against drinking at a bar. But there was a law that prohibited running a gambling operation, and that's what Trozzo was doing. He wasn't even hiding it.

Stanard walked over to Trozzo. "What the hell is wrong with you?" he said. "We specifically told you to stay out of Otto's. People don't want you here. Now we got a complaint about you."

Trozzo looked around, apparently trying to figure out who the hell had ratted him out. "I didn't know the place was hot. Honest."

"Oh, come on, Trozzo. Don't give me that line."

"This is a big day," Trozzo said, reasoning with Stanard. "I'll give you a hundred bucks from today's take."

"A hundred," Stanard repeated with a tone of disgust.

"Okay, okay, four hundred," Trozzo told him.

"That's better," Stanard said. "But we had a complaint, so we still have to take you in. Don't sweat it; we'll go easy on you."

Frank kept his mouth shut—this wasn't his arrest—but the whole scene was far too predictable.

The next morning, Frank ran into Stanard in the plainclothes office at the 48th Precinct.

"That lying bastard Trozzo," Stanard said, leaning back in his chair. "He only came up with two bills because I booked him."

He extended a folded hundred-dollar bill to Frank, but Frank didn't take it.

"Keep it," Frank said. "You did all the work; it was your collar."

Stanard flipped his thumb toward the door. "Let's go for a ride."

They walked out of the precinct and got into an unmarked car.

"This is an opportunity," Stanard said as they cruised through the neighborhood. "You can make easy money. I'm talking eight hundred a month, maybe more. I made sixty thousand dollars in two years, and that's just off the pad."

"I'm okay without it," Frank said.

The two cops drove in silence for a few minutes.

"Y'know, Frank, we got a call about you. The guy didn't give his name, but he said you couldn't be trusted."

"Why's that? Because I don't take money?"

"Yeah, probably. But I told them you were okay. I said we used to work together at the Seven-O. I mean, you're weird, the way you dress and you hanging out in the Village and stuff, but you're all right."

Then Stanard told Frank that the cops in the 7th Division weren't doing anything wrong. "They just skim some money off a gambling house," he said. "The bosses pay it willingly. To them it's just the cost of doing business."

"I don't care what you guys are up to," Frank said. "I just do my own thing." What he didn't say was that doing his own thing included monitoring the precinct's crooked operation.

"Well, if you don't like it, speak with me. I can get you transferred. Maybe you'd rather work in Times Square and arrest prostitutes."

There was nothing Frank wanted less. This time, he wanted to stay. Now he wanted to be around the crooked cops.

Now he was taking notes.

– Let Me Explain –

At this point, you're probably wondering why the hell I didn't just leave the force. Looking back, I ask myself the same question. But until I took that envelope from Jewish Max, I had no idea how bad things were. I figured there might be a rogue cop or two, but I didn't think the system was rotten to the core.

Also, at that age, I was naive enough to believe the bosses would want to fix the problem. I was convinced I could find someone in the force who didn't know about the pad—the money the cops were skimming. I figured that once I shed some light on the problem, there'd be a major investigation, and the department would get a thorough cleaning out.

I was wrong.

Thinking about it now, I realize how alone I was. All those guys cared about was keeping the pad, and they tried every which way to justify their actions. I remember one cop suggesting I take the bribes and put the money in the poor box at church. He saw it as doing a good deed.

"Dirty money in the poor box?" I said. "Where the hell is your conscience?"

The other thing you have to understand is that the cops didn't like that I wanted to be left alone. It really bothered them; they were scared I would turn them in. They didn't trust me.

Keep reading and you'll see what I mean.

Chapter Three

FOR THE COPS WORKING THE 7TH DIVISION, LIFE WAS GOOD.

Nobody told them what to do or paid much attention to their comings and goings. While on duty, they'd head to the movies, hang out in bars, or, for those who lived in the suburbs, gather at one another's houses to swim in their pools or cook steaks on their barbecues. They had to phone the station house regularly, but the switchboard was rarely monitored.

To Frank, it seemed the only assignment they took seriously was collecting the pad and serving their racketeer clients. Every now and then, they'd make a "clean" arrest, nothing major, just enough to keep things looking legitimate.

Dammit, they could be good cops. They had connections. They knew how to solve crimes. If they'd wanted to, they could've cleaned up the entire district in no time.

Frank continued to put in an honest day's work, staying clear of any shenanigans, and was surprised when one of the boys from the 7th Division, Carmello Zumatto, asked him if he wanted in on the pad. They were having a drink at Zumatto's place in the Bronx, an apartment he kept strictly for socializing—and had no doubt paid for with dirty money.

Zumatto sat on the couch, reached under a cushion, and pulled out a fat envelope with the division's monthly take. He started counting the contents.

"Well?" Zumatto said. "Are you in?"

Frank looked at Zumatto, his fleshy face, his round eyes. Hadn't the guy heard that Frank wasn't one of the boys?

"Nah," Frank said. "You can do whatever you want. Just keep me out of it."

"I understand," Zumatto said, nodding. "Here's what I'll do. I'll count out your share and save it for you. If you ever want it, just come by and pick it up. Sound good?"

"Like I said, do whatever you want, but I don't want it."

After that, Zumatto stopped asking Frank to take the money, but kept on doing it himself.

On one ride, Frank and Zumatto followed up on a letter sent to the precinct by the mother of a teenage boy. The woman was worried that her son was getting caught up in the numbers racket. She thought he might be working for Brook Sims, a local gambling boss. In all likelihood, her kid was one of the runners who carried the money and betting slips to Sims's headquarters.

Frank and Zumatto drove in an unmarked car to the block where Sims usually worked. When they spotted him making his rounds, Zumatto turned to Frank. "Let's grab him."

They cornered Sims and frisked him. The guy had enough betting slips on him to qualify as a felony arrest.

"Whoa, whoa," Sims said, clearly confused. "What's up? Aren't you with the division? I took care of you guys already."

Zumatto told Sims they'd received a complaint from somebody in the neighborhood. "We're gonna have to take you in."

"Jesus, I can't go now," Sims said. "I'm losing money just standing here. Can I meet you at the precinct? Give me a few hours. I'll be there at four thirty."

"Okay," Zumatto said. "But be there on time. Don't make us come looking for you."

On the ride back, Frank asked Zumatto what the hell was going on. "Are you kidding me? You let the guy decide when he's going to be arrested?"

"Relax, Frank," Zumatto said. "Sims is okay, he'll turn up. He always does. We'll make a show of arresting him, and he'll be out in the morning. Everybody wins."

But in Frank's mind, everybody lost; Sims would be back on the street, and that mother's boy would still be running numbers.

Zumatto had been right about one thing: Sims did show up on time. At four thirty on the nose, he walked into the precinct with a batch of betting slips in his pocket. Only this time, he didn't have as many as before. So he couldn't be tagged with a felony. Instead, Zumatto charged him with a misdemeanor, and sure enough, the case was dropped the next day. This was how the system worked: The police made thousands of arrests every year, but small-time crooks would barely get a slap on the wrist—only a third of them wound up getting convicted.

One day, when Zumatto was tied up in court, Frank partnered with Robert Stanard, the guy who had brought Frank to Otto's Bar and Grill to shake down Pasquale Trozzo. Together, they drove to a house on a residential block in the South Bronx.

Stanard guided the cruiser to the curb; a man came out of a two-story red-brick house and walked over to the driver's side of the patrol car. Stanard rolled down the window.

"This is Frank," Stanard said, wagging his thumb in Frank's direction. "He's all right, he's one of us."

The man, who was Puerto Rican, shook Frank's hand.

"Listen," Stanard told him. "The precinct is watching you. They've got warrants out on your candy store and the tailor shop."

"Oh, Christ, thanks for letting me know," he said. "I'll stop taking bets until things cool off."

After the man went back inside, Stanard looked at the house and shook his head in disgust. "That cheap bastard," he said, driving off.

"If he was a wop, he'd have been good for something, maybe a fifty or, at the very least, a nice bottle of Scotch."

Stanard obviously knew that "wop" was a derogatory term for a person of Italian descent, but he didn't seem to care that he'd just insulted Frank's ancestry. Even more surprising to Frank was that Stanard cared about a free bottle of booze. By 1967, New York City patrolmen earned about $8,000 a year, and with overtime Stanard could get that number up to five figures. It was a decent living, quite a bit higher than the average American salary and in line with firefighters and teachers.

So why did guys like Stanard want every last dirty penny?

Frank had stopped asking, because the answers usually boiled down to the cops feeling entitled to it. And the answers were getting predictable. *We work hard. The money's dirty, anyway. It's not like we're hurting anybody.*

But that wasn't true, and Stanard had to know it. These gambling bosses were also destroying the lives of children, teenagers, and entire families by putting drugs like heroin on the street. Frank couldn't let them off the hook—not with a clean conscience.

The Roots of Corruption

In this 1895 political cartoon, the Washington Post *decries Mayor Strong hurriedly pulling Theodore Roosevelt away from his civil service post in the nation's capital to reform New York's finest.*

Since the New York City Police Department was formed in 1845, the pad was as much a part of policing as a brass button.

Near the end of the nineteenth century, corruption was so out of hand that the New York State Senate formed a committee to investigate wrongdoing in the department. The Lexow Committee's report found that city cops regularly demanded payments from brothels, bars, pool halls, and gambling joints. It was a multimillion-dollar-a-year system that put money in the pockets of cops, from lowly patrolmen to high-ranking inspectors.

One of the most damning pieces of evidence came from Thomas Byrnes, the superintendent of the NYPD. Byrnes testified that he was worth $350,000, the equivalent of nearly $12 million today. How did a public official, on a salary of $5,000 a year, become so rich? Byrnes said that

Cornelius Vanderbilt and Jay Gould, two of the wealthiest men in America, had invested his money for him. It just so happened that Byrnes had a shady relationship with both men, having kept labor unions from gaining traction in their workplaces.

A few months after the committee issued its report, Mayor William Strong appointed Theodore Roosevelt president of the city's Board of Police Commissioners. When taking the job, Roosevelt wrote to his sister Anna, "I have the most important, and the most corrupt, department in New York on my hands . . . and I know well how hard the task ahead of me is."

Roosevelt's first move was to accept Byrnes's resignation. Then he got rid of any cops who'd been caught taking bribes and enticed veteran officers to retire. He personally went around the city looking for patrolmen who were sleeping on the job or spending their shifts at bars. And he did away with patronage. Officers could no longer bribe their way up the ladder; they would have to earn their promotions by proving themselves worthy.

After two years, Roosevelt left the post to become assistant secretary of the navy; he later became the twenty-sixth president of the United States.

Frank believed the police department could be cleaned up, but he couldn't do it alone. He had to catch the ear of a supervisor who had the guts to change things, not a puppet like Foran.

Unlike Durk, Frank wasn't connected. But he did know a guy who might be able to help.

When he was filing fingerprints at the Bureau of Criminal Identification, Frank had met a captain named Cornelius Behan. Now they were both taking criminology classes at John Jay College of Police Science. Frank was aware of Behan's rank: He was an administrator in the public morals division of the Chief Inspector's Office.

A guy in that position had to have contacts high up in the department, so Frank took a chance. The next time he ran into Behan, he told him the basics: The cops at the 7th Division were dirty; they were taking payoffs. Frank wanted somebody to do something about it.

"Do you have time to talk?"

"Sure, but you're dealing with a very delicate topic," Behan said, looking up and down the corridor.

This wasn't a conversation for a public hallway, especially one filled with cops who were going to night school.

"I've got my car," Frank said. "Can we go there and talk?"

"Perfect," Behan said. "I've got to catch a train after class. If you meet me at the corner of Thirteenth and Fourth, you can drive me to Penn Station."

"I'll be there."

Frank watched as Behan strode down the corridor. The guy had the look of a cop—gray herringbone overcoat, gray fedora, square attaché case—but he seemed to be a straight shooter. Frank trusted him.

He had no choice.

That night, Frank sat in his car at the corner of 13th Street and 4th Avenue with the engine idling. Behan showed up right on time, and Frank eased the car down a dimly lit side street and double-parked.

"The Seventh Division is dirty," he said, not wasting any time. "For that matter, so is every other plainclothes detail I've been assigned to since I got out of the academy."

He went on from there, telling Behan how the cops in the division were splitting the pad and how they each took home at least $800 a month in bribe money.

Every cop, that is, except Frank.

"Who are we talking about?" Behan said. "Can you give me names?"

Frank shook his head. "I'm not going to do that. This isn't about nailing a few corrupt officers. It's about the entire system. It goes all the way up the ladder."

Behan stayed silent; he seemed to be digesting what he'd just heard. Finally, he spoke. "Hang in there. I'll get a meeting with John Walsh soon. We'll see what he has to say about this."

When they reached Penn Station, Behan got out of the car telling Frank he'd be in touch. But his words hung in the air long after he was gone.

John Walsh?

Frank couldn't have asked for more. Walsh was the second most powerful cop in the city. He answered to nobody except the commissioner, Howard Leary. Walsh had made a name for himself by spying on dirty cops. The *New York Times* called him "the biggest shoo-fly of them all." Commissioners came and went, but Walsh stayed put—quietly and carefully doing a job other cops didn't want to do.

Police Commissioner Howard Leary

John Walsh, first deputy commissioner

Most everybody in blue knew Walsh's story. He'd started as a beat cop and worked his way up to second-in-command. If he found out that an officer was profiting from the job, he wouldn't hesitate before taking away the guy's gun and badge.

It was hard to imagine that Walsh wouldn't want to clean up the force once and for all.

Behan kept his word and, in February 1967, called Frank.

"Frank, I've got good news for you," he said. "I met with Walsh and he's thrilled to hear a man of integrity has surfaced. He said he's impressed that you're willing to come forward. He's been waiting for somebody like you."

This was even better than Frank had hoped.

"I'm glad to hear that," Frank said. "When can I meet with him?"

"He considered moving you out of the Seventh Division and into anticorruption," Behan said. "But he thinks it's smarter to leave things as they are so you can keep on gathering information."

"With all due respect, Captain, I've already said I don't want to incriminate fellow officers. I want to meet with Walsh as soon as possible, so I can explain what's going on. It's not just the Seventh Division. The whole department's broken and needs to be investigated from the ground up."

Frank waited for an answer, but none came. He could practically hear Behan thinking.

"Well, Captain?"

"Sit tight, Frank. I'll be in touch."

Behan hung up.

So Frank stayed at the 7th Division, smack in the middle of the shakedowns and the payoffs, but he tried to see the positives. At least he had put his complaint on the record with a top official. Also,

Behan didn't say Walsh wouldn't meet with him. He only said he wouldn't meet with him *yet*.

A few weeks later, Behan phoned Frank and said to meet him Sunday afternoon on the Exit 10 ramp off the Van Wyck Expressway in Queens. Frank was practically salivating. If Behan wanted to meet, he must have gotten hold of some good information.

Sunday brought with it a cold, wet rain. Frank left his apartment and trotted to his car. With him was David Durk, who had insisted on coming along.

"I'm part of this, too," Durk had said.

That wasn't entirely true; it was Frank who had put himself in the department's crosshairs. But bringing Durk did have its benefits, the most important of which was that Frank would have a witness to the meeting.

When Frank and Durk drove onto the exit ramp, Behan was waiting. He had parked his car on the shoulder of the road and was leaning on the front fender, seemingly oblivious to the light drizzle that was dampening the rim of his hat and the shoulders of his overcoat.

Frank pulled up behind him and got out, leaving Durk sitting in the passenger's seat with the wipers running. The air smelled of damp tar and car fumes.

"What the hell?" Behan said to Frank, nodding toward Durk. "I pick an out-of-the-way place so nobody can see us, and you show up with a friend? Don't you know the first damned thing about the word 'undercover'?"

"He's with me," Frank said, raising his voice to be heard over the speeding cars on the highway below. "We can trust him."

"I don't care if he's George Washington. I'm meeting with you, not him."

"Well, we're here now."

"Okay, okay, here's the deal," said Behan, obviously still annoyed.

"I told Walsh what you told me. He wants you to stay on at the division. Just keep at it."

"I'll do whatever he feels is best. But I thought you asked me here to tell me something new."

"It is new," Behan snapped. "Because Walsh just said it."

"Well, sir, I'm a little nervous about meeting you like this while I'm still working at the division. If word ever got out . . ."

"How the hell is word going to get out? You're the guy who's bringing friends to meetings."

Frank stayed silent and Behan took a breath.

"Look," Behan said. "Walsh will see you whenever and wherever you want. Just name the place. He'll meet you at the last station of any subway in the goddamned city. That's how committed he is to protecting your identity."

"Yeah, okay, okay."

"But for now, go back to work and keep your eyes open," Behan said. "Walsh will be in touch."

He got in his car and drove off. Frank walked back to Durk, who was itching to hear what happened.

"Well?" Durk said.

"I guess I'm working for Walsh undercover," Frank said. "I'd like to meet with the guy, but what other choice do I have?"

As they headed back to Manhattan, Frank tried to process what had just happened. Reporting on colleagues was the work of whistleblowers—and crooks hate whistleblowers. But Frank didn't see himself as blowing the whistle. He saw himself as a "lamp lighter," a person who shines a light on things that are wrong.

"There's one problem," he said to Durk. "You know what happens to whistleblowers. I could wind up with a bullet in my head."

Durk ducked the issue. But he reminded Frank that when the deputy commissioner of police asks you to do something, it's a good idea to do it.

– Why It Mattered –

I know what you're thinking: This guy had a mark on his back. Why didn't he just ignore the payouts, let cops like Stanard stash their dirty money, and keep on doing his job? Or, even easier, why didn't he just quit?

Well, first of all, we're not talking about a few rogue cops around the city getting a cut of some gambling money. We're talking about an organized system of corruption that ran all the way up to the top of the NYPD. That was my great revelation: that no one in the department I told about the corruption was surprised, and that nobody wanted to stop it. The top cops—the brass, as we used to say—knew what was going on and were allowing it to happen. Remember Arnold Fraiman? The guy we weren't going to call because Durk didn't know him well enough? Well, eventually we sat down with him. The City Commissioner of Investigation would agree to bug the apartment, but then tell Durk—behind my back— that he thought I was a psycho.

It was a cheap move, because he knew the department was basically another form of organized crime, another mob. Except mobsters don't pretend they're something other than what they are.

So think about your question again. What was at stake for me to keep fighting against the system? My character, my reputation. Had I let them intimidate me, had I taken that dirty money, who would I be when I looked in the mirror? How could I have walked away when kids' lives were at stake? What would my father have thought of the man I'd become?

No, I wasn't about to give in. No way, no how.

Chapter Four

IN OCTOBER 1967, FRANK WAS IN THE BRONX, WORKING plainclothes and keeping his eye on the pad, just as Walsh had directed through Behan.

One day, he found himself sitting in front of Deputy Chief Inspector Stephen Killorin, the commander of the 7th Division. When he'd walked into Killorin's office, he had no idea why he'd been summoned, but he was getting up to speed in a hurry.

"Why the hell didn't you come to me?" Killorin said, his chiseled features getting sharper as he shouted. "What do you think? You're the only honest guy here?"

Frank shifted in his chair. "I wasn't getting any support, sir."

"So where did you go, Serpico? Who have you spoken to?"

Obviously, word was out in the division that Frank was complaining about other cops. But how much Killorin knew was anybody's guess. The last thing Frank wanted to do was tell the inspector that he'd met with Foran at the DOI and was now waiting for a face-to-face with Walsh. Or that he and Durk had also met with Jay Kriegel, chief of staff to Mayor Lindsay. Kriegel hadn't done much; he'd sent Frank word that Lindsay didn't want to get involved, that an investigation would strain the mayor's relationship with the police. But Killorin wouldn't wait for the details. He'd think the DOI was trouble—and the mayor's office radioactive.

Frank chose his words carefully. "Nothing was getting done here," he said. "I had no choice."

"To do what? Don't tell me you've gone to any outside agencies. We clean our own laundry around here."

"Honestly, Inspector, I don't see anybody cleaning up anything. The cops in this division are taking payoffs, and nobody's stopping them. And we're not talking run-of-the-mill stuff. This place is as crooked as the gambling houses we're supposed to be shutting down. It's like these guys have a second job."

Killorin sat silently, his jaw tight. "What agencies have you gone to?" Apparently, the only thing that mattered to him was what might show up in the press.

"That's not important," Frank said. "This isn't about public relations. It's about cleaning up the force."

"The hell it's not about public relations," Killorin said. "Give me the names of the cops."

"I can't do that."

"Why not?" Killorin said. "Isn't that your whole point?"

"No, sir. I want to change the system. I'm not out to get one or two guys."

"You're going around blabbing that plainclothes is filled with corruption, but you won't give me names? How the hell am I supposed to investigate that?"

Killorin had a point.

"I'll give you four gambling operators," Frank said. "Check with them—they're not afraid. They'll tell you they're paying cops and that they've been doing it for years."

Killorin didn't seem happy, but he took down the information. Then he walked Frank to the door. "From now on," he said, "keep things under this roof."

"I will," Frank lied. Why should he keep his mouth shut? He was clean. If anybody should be afraid of the press, it was the crooked cops, not him.

"All right," Killorin said. "I'm going to pair you up with Jules Sachson. He's the inspector in charge of public morals here in the Bronx. You can work with him on this corruption business."

With that, the meeting ended.

It wasn't long before Frank was in Sachson's car on 19th Street in Manhattan, a block from the West Side Highway.

Inspector Jules Sachson

Sachson, a heavy guy with a receding hairline and V-shaped eyebrows, sat behind the wheel, telling Frank he sympathized with him. "This must be a strain on you," he said, his meaty hands resting on the steering wheel.

"Damned right it is," Frank said. "For the life of me, I can't understand how it winds up that the dirty cops are putting pressure on the clean ones, and not the other way around."

"I've been asking that same question for years," Sachson said, nodding. Then he ticked off a few of his previous successes fighting police corruption.

"You've got a good reputation," Frank said. "But believe me, what's going on in the Bronx isn't anything you've seen before. These guys are running a high-stakes side business. Right out in the open."

"We'll bring 'em down," Sachson said, taking out a notepad. "Who are they? How many are we talking?"

Frank shook his head. "I already told Killorin that I'm not gonna tag any cops. You'll have to figure that part out on your own."

Sachson gripped the notepad in one hand and a pen in the other. "Serpico," he said, "at some point, you're going to have to trust somebody."

It was true, Frank couldn't fight the entire department on his own. Sooner or later, he'd have to trust somebody. Why not Sachson? He came across as an ethical guy. He seemed to understand Frank. Sachson himself had fought corruption; he'd gone after crooked cops. Maybe the time had come to spill the whole deal.

"Here goes," Frank said.

As Sachson scribbled on his notepad, Frank reeled off a list of guys: Stanard, Zumatto, and others. He named the lieutenant who had offered him a place to stash dirty money, and another who'd said he knew about the pad. Then he threw in thirty-six gambling operations that were paying off the 7th Division. He kept going until Sachson's notepad was covered in names, dates, and places.

Saying it all aloud was a relief, but the reality turned his stomach.

Sachson looked at Frank and let out a long, slow whistle. "That's some list. I think our best bet is for you to wear a wire."

Frank had seen this coming and already had an answer. He wasn't about to walk through the 7th Division, or ride alongside other cops, with a recorder taped to his body. That stuff was for the feds—and besides, if he got caught, he was dead meat.

"There's no way I'm gonna do that," he said. "I know what you're going to do. You're going to charge a couple of cops and tell the press you got the bad guys. Applause, applause, applause. Meanwhile, the guys on top will drive back to their million-dollar homes."

"Not true."

"It's damned well true," Frank said. "And it's been happening for a hundred years. This kind of corruption goes way up the chain. I'm not gonna help you bring down a couple of patsies who are putting in a day's work, as dirty as it might be, so that you or Killorin can beef up your résumés. Because if that happens, you'll have failed."

Sachson didn't answer, so as far as Frank was concerned, the wire issue was closed.

But the flames were getting higher. The rumors circulating through the division were now true: Somebody really was telling stories about bad cops.

And the cops in the Bronx had to know it was Frank.

One of the gambling locations that Frank gave to Sachson was a bodega at 920 East Tremont Avenue, not far from the Cross Bronx Expressway. The owners, he said, were a married couple named Juan and Dolores Carreras. The Carrerases were taking bets at their store, but they'd never been arrested because they'd been dutifully paying protection money to the cops every month.

Sachson proved he was worthy of Frank's trust. Months later, they met on East Tremont, a sorry stretch of abandoned storefronts, gated windows, and broken sidewalks. On the corner of Daly Avenue sat the bodega, which, in street terms, was also a policy shop—a place where people went to place bets.

This is where the Carrerases took numbers.

Frank looked at the place. The gambling bosses had dozens of these shops across the Bronx. They'd set up their operations in bodegas, candy stores, and other local businesses. Then they'd make a fortune while the shop owners, people like the Carrerases, got only a tiny sliver of the pie.

Frank and Sachson found Dolores Carreras behind the counter, working alone. The air smelled of boiled hot dogs and stale coffee.

Sachson held up a search warrant. "We have it on good authority that you're taking numbers."

"And?" Carreras said.

"And we're here to search the place."

"Go ahead," she said.

Sachson kept his eye on Carreras so that Frank could rummage through the shop. Frank peeked behind the counter, took a look inside the cash register, and then checked the freezer. It wasn't long before he found stacks of policy slips, the stubs indicating the numbers people had bet on the next day's lottery. First, he pulled a bunch of them from behind the freezer. Then he found more piles inside the storeroom, lying out in the open. Apparently, Carreras didn't feel she had anything to hide.

When Frank walked out of the storeroom with the slips, Sachson's eyes lit up. "Are those what I think they are?"

"Yep."

Police raid a policy shop in Brooklyn.

Dolores Carreras looked at Frank and shrugged her shoulders, as if he'd just walked out of the storeroom holding nothing but a quart of milk.

"Book her," Sachson said to Frank. Then he turned to Carreras. "Did you really think we wouldn't check back there?"

"What are you even doing here?" she said. "Didn't you get your share?"

"Share of what?" Sachson said.

Carreras didn't answer. Instead, she just looked straight ahead, her lips tight.

Frank and Sachson drove her to the station house, and once there, they arrested her and took her prints. As Frank rolled the tips of her inked fingers onto the print card, Carreras looked at him, a bewildered expression on her face.

"I can't believe this," she said, her voice sounding more nervous than it had back at the store. "Why don't you take the money like the other cops?"

Frank kept on inking her prints. "What makes you think I don't?"

"Because, if you did, you wouldn't be arresting me."

Sachson jumped into the conversation, his voice casual but his question loaded. "So you pay cops not to arrest you? Is that what you're telling us?"

"Not me, my husband."

"Who does he pay?" Sachson said.

"Stanard," she said. "And Zumatto. Sometimes Paretti."

Sachson shot Frank a quick glance. They were the same names Frank had given him.

Being proved right did nothing for Frank. As Frank predicted, the dirty cops—in this case, Stanard, Zumatto, and James Paretti—would wind up taking the fall for all the other guys on the pad, especially the higher-ups. And Frank would get dragged into the muck.

The only question was when it would happen.

The Numbers Racket

New York City plainclothesmen stake out a gambling operation in 1964.

In the 1960s, neighborhoods throughout New York City were filled with illegal betting operations. Residents could place bets in a number of local establishments, such as pizza parlors, candy stores, bodegas, and bars. Most often they bet on sporting events or on a game known as the numbers.

To play the numbers, a bettor would write a three-digit number on a slip of paper, hoping it would match a number drawn at random the next day. The odds were a thousand to one against winning, but the game was tempting, since picking the right number could pay as much as $600 on a $1 bet.

A bettor could risk as little as a nickel, which is why some people referred to the racket as the poor man's lottery. Everybody could play. And apparently, everybody did, especially in low-income neighborhoods, where desperation ran high. By the mid-1960s, the NYPD estimated that more than half a million New Yorkers played the numbers every day—spending at least $200 million a year.

In May, Frank got a call from Bronx District Attorney Burton Roberts. There was nothing calm about Roberts. He had a short fuse and a fiery temper, and his voice was once described as being a few decibels below the roar of a jet engine.

Roberts asked Frank to have a private meeting with him and gave Frank the name, address, and room number of a motel in the Bronx.

Frank could just imagine what the DA was going to say. Roberts was probably mounting a case against a few cops and wanted Frank to help him fill in the blanks. It was low-level stuff, and Frank was tired of it.

When Frank entered the motel room, he found Roberts huddled with a handful of staff members. Roberts shook his hand and told Frank how much he admired him.

"We're grateful to you for coming forward," he said. "It's rare to find a policeman willing to stick his neck out like this."

"Thanks," Frank said guardedly, knowing Roberts hadn't set up the meeting just to pat him on the back.

"Tell me what's going on at the Seventh Division," Roberts said. "Pretend I don't know anything, and give me the whole story from start to finish."

"You already know the highlights," Frank said. "What more do you want?"

Bronx DA Burton Roberts

"We're putting together a case against Stanard, Zumatto, and Paretti," Roberts said. "But it's not going to be easy. All three of them have clean records. Frank, I need you to testify in front of the grand jury."

There it was. Just as Frank had suspected, Roberts had an ulterior motive. And Frank didn't like it.

"Go to hell," Frank said.

But Roberts refused to back down. "You don't have to worry about being singled out. We're going to call a bunch of cops from the Seventh Division. Nobody will know what you said or didn't say."

"This is a sham," Frank said. He knew grand juries were meant to be held in secret, but if he opened his mouth in court, it wouldn't take long for word to get out. And a lot of crooked cops would want to even the score.

He left the motel figuring he wouldn't have to testify. But Roberts wouldn't give up. He summoned Frank to a second meeting, this time in the apartment of one of Roberts's assistant DAs.

Roberts sat in an overstuffed armchair, puffing on a cigar. As he flicked the ashes into a glass dish, he explained why he needed Frank's help. Again, Frank refused, pointing to his frustration with the department.

"I've spent months waiting for Walsh to do something," he said. "This is chickenshit."

"Hold on," Roberts said. "What's your problem with Walsh?"

At this point, Frank had nothing to lose. He told Roberts how he'd reported the corruption in the 7th Division to Walsh through Behan. And he told him how he hadn't heard a single word in response.

"Fine," Roberts said. "I'll put you on the stand; you say what you know, and I'll show the grand jury how much is at stake. I'll show them that the corruption goes all the way up the chain of command. We'll investigate the whole department. We'll turn the entire city upside down and clean it from top to bottom. But we need you,

Frank. With you on the stand, we can turn this whole thing around. Just tell the grand jury what you know."

Roberts seemed to mean what he said, that he would go after the department and not a couple of two-bit cops. And so Frank agreed to testify and hoped for the best.

He also knew that, in agreeing to talk, he'd become a marked man. Convinced he was being followed, he began carrying a second gun, a Browning semiautomatic. It was hard to miss the irony. Frank had needed only one gun to chase down criminals, but he doubly armed himself to stay safe from the police.

On June 26, 1968, Frank sat in the Bronx Supreme Court testifying in front of the grand jury, ready to sink the entire department. But every question put to him had to do with plainclothes cops; not one had to do with superior officers. All the DA wanted to know, or all he wanted the grand jury to hear, was how Frank's fellow cops worked the pad.

Under oath, Frank answered the questions to the best of his knowledge and went home, adding Roberts to the list of powerful officials who had spewed false promises.

He kept on working at the 7th Division while the grand jury hearings continued through the summer and into the fall. In November, Stanard testified twice, both times denying any underhanded dealings with gambling bosses.

In December, Frank was transferred out of the division and sent to plainclothes duty in Manhattan North, which primarily covered Harlem.

On his first day, he walked into the main room of the precinct and saw a dozen or so cops standing around drinking coffee and gabbing. All of them ignored Frank except for one, a plainclothesman with curly black hair and blue eyes.

The guy walked over to Frank and pulled out a switchblade. Staring Frank in the eye, he held it in his hand, unopened, and wagged it back and forth. His message was clear: You testified against us; you're going to pay.

The room went silent. Frank could see the other cops watching him, smirking, waiting to see how he'd react.

"We know how to handle guys like you," the black-haired cop said. He pressed a button on the knife and a blade popped out, emitting a distinctive click. "I ought to cut your tongue out."

In a flash, Frank raised his left forearm and smacked it against the guy's wrist, a martial-arts move he'd learned when studying goju-ryu years earlier. The knife flew out of the cop's hand, clattering across the floor.

Frank grabbed his other wrist and twisted it back, hard. The guy screamed, but Frank showed little mercy. He kept on twisting until the cop was doubled over. When he finally let go, he shoved the guy backward with his leg, sending the cop to the floor like a first-time roller skater.

Whipping out his semiautomatic, Frank pressed it against the cop's head. "Move a muscle, and I swear on my mother I'll blow your brains out."

The only sound in the room was the hum of the coffee machine.

Frank stole a quick glance at the other plainclothesmen. No one was smirking any longer.

Finally, one of them coughed nervously. "Jesus Christ, Serpico, is that a forty-five?"

Frank shook his head. "No, nine millimeter."

"Oh, yeah, the new Browning. How many rounds does it hold?"

"Fourteen," Frank said, keeping his eyes, and his gun, trained on the cop's forehead.

"Wow, that's a lot. What do you need fourteen rounds for?"

"How many guys you got in this precinct?" Frank asked.

"Oh, hey, we were just joking."

"Yeah, so was I," Frank said, pulling the gun away and getting up. Then he walked to his locker, leaving the cop on the floor.

Frank was immediately shuttled off to temporary duty with the 18th Precinct. The One-Eight was on West 54th Street in Midtown, just north of Times Square. Now Frank was no longer working gambling houses. His assignment was vice, which meant he'd be arresting prostitutes.

The job allowed Frank to work undercover. He didn't love it, but he became an expert at disguises. He walked his beat in elaborate costumes he dreamed up in his apartment. Using props such as a bowler, a beret, eyeglasses, pipes, and a cane, he became Max the German beer salesman or Carlos the Spanish industrialist. Donning one of his favorite disguises—a long beard, black hat, and ankle-length overcoat—he transformed himself into an Amish farmer.

But the assignment didn't last long, and Frank returned to Manhattan North. This time, having seen his martial arts skills, the cops at the precinct left him alone.

On February 11, the grand jury handed up indictments against eight policemen from Frank's old detail in the 7th Division. The names Robert Stanard, Carmello Zumatto, and James Paretti were right there in black-and-white newsprint for the world to see. All eight cops were being indicted for lying to the grand jury and immediately suspended. But just as Frank suspected, guys like Foran and Behan got off scot-free. There were no indictments against them or any other higher-ups for turning a blind eye to corruption. The grand jury had done exactly as Frank had predicted. The district attorney had gone after the flunkies and let the brass walk away, unscathed.

In his press conference following the announcement, District Attorney Roberts said that major gambling operations would be hobbled without the likes of Stanard, Zumatto, and Paretti protecting them. Roberts kept Frank's name out of the papers, but every cop knew the source of the leak. The DA had done exactly what Frank had asked him not to do: He'd put a target on Frank's back.

It was then that fate intervened in the form of his new boss at Manhattan North, Inspector Paul Delise.

The inspector was a short, compact man with a soft voice that belied the power of his position. When Frank walked into his office

Paul Delise (far right) oversees a marijuana bust in Queens.

for the first time, he could only imagine what Delise was thinking. Here was this whack job Serpico, wearing an army jacket, his hair hanging over his ears, his beard grown out, and his feet, sockless, in sandals. At first sight, Delise probably thought he was a suspect ready to be fingerprinted.

Frank introduced himself. "Officer Serpico, sir."

"I know who you are," Delise said.

Of course he did. Every cop in the city had heard about the indictments.

Delise pointed toward a chair. It was an invitation to sit, and Frank took it. After a few formalities, Frank launched into his predicament. He told Delise he was an outcast, that he couldn't find a partner, and that he'd never wanted to testify in the first place.

Delise seemed sympathetic. "You might not believe this, Frank, but I'm happy to have you here," he said. "We need men with your integrity."

Frank wasn't looking for a pep talk. He'd been down that road before. "That's great," he said. "If you find another guy with integrity, you can make him my partner."

Delise paused for a moment, then nodded. "I'll do it."

Frank considered the offer. Delise was nearly fifty. His days of climbing rooftops and sneaking down alleyways were long since over.

"Are you serious?" Frank said.

"Absolutely. I'll be your partner."

"You sure about that?"

"I'm sure," Delise said.

Again, Frank thought about it, but the bottom line was that he had no other offers. "You've got a deal."

The two men worked side by side through the summer of 1969. Delise was a crackerjack cop—seasoned, enthusiastic, and prepared. He carried a duffel bag filled with cameras, recording devices, walkie-talkies, and binoculars.

Together, Frank and Delise developed a routine. Frank would climb onto a rooftop and use the binoculars to keep an eye out for suspicious activity. When he spotted a policy shop, he'd go in for the bust, swooping through skylights, barreling down stairs, cutting through alleys. Delise would wait outside while the action was taking place and then serve as Frank's backup.

One night, Frank and Delise identified what looked to be a major gambling operation on the ground floor of a six-story building in Harlem. The setup was simple but safe: The bosses had a guy stationed outside the building. He was the lookout. If trouble was brewing, he would signal the men inside.

Frank, working on the street instead of a rooftop, couldn't get past the lookout. Infuriated, he spotted a garbage can, picked it up, flung it through a plate-glass window, and then jumped into the building. Drawing his gun, he held four guys at bay while letting Delise in through the side door. Then he and Delise called for backup, but their walkie-talkies jammed.

Frank wasn't about to give up. With Delise now training his gun on the suspects, Frank snuck out the side door into a blind alley, climbed up to the roof, ran down the fire escape on the far side of the building, and called for help from a pay phone.

When they got back to the precinct, Delise looked at Frank and shook his head. "I always knew you had integrity. But I never knew you had a death wish."

"What are you talking about?" Frank said, but he knew what Delise meant.

He always picked the most dangerous route to safety.

Two and a half years had passed since Frank first met with Behan, and despite all of the captain's promises, Frank still hadn't heard from Deputy Commissioner Walsh.

While waiting, Frank continued to gather evidence and make nothing but enemies in the department. There was only so long he could maintain the operation—if it even was an operation—before an angry cop would put a bullet in his head.

Frank had one move left, but he'd been avoiding it. He had to go outside the department. He had to let people in the city know what was happening. Not only would such a move get Walsh to act more quickly, but it might also protect Frank. If he could get his story in the newspaper, the cops wouldn't dare arrest him, or shoot him, or run him out of the force. How could they? Everybody would know where to find the culprits.

So in the middle of 1969, Frank called David Durk and asked him if he had any contacts in the press.

"Yeah, I know a guy at the *Times*," Durk said. "But you sure you want to make this call?"

It was obvious why Durk was asking. The *New York Times* had nearly a million readers; it was the country's most powerful and influential paper. Anyone of any importance read it. If the *Times* published Frank's story, all hell would break loose, and there'd be no turning back.

"I have no other choice," Frank said.

"Then let's do it."

Within days, Durk set up a meeting at a Greenwich Village coffee shop with his friend David Burnham. An investigative reporter for the *Times* who covered law enforcement, Burnham had spent the previous December digging into the practice of cooping. Along with a photographer, he'd driven around the city in the middle of the night, searching for policemen sleeping on the job. They'd snapped photos of uniformed cops napping in their patrol cars and snoozing in parks. Some even had pillows and alarm clocks.

When Burnham's article had run on the front page of the *Times*, New Yorkers couldn't help but ask: Who was policing the police?

Frank had seen the article, so when he walked into the luncheonette to meet Burnham, he figured he was in good hands. After all, Burnham had already reported on delinquent cops. Why wouldn't he do it again?

The three men grabbed a quiet table. Once their mugs were filled with hot coffee, Burnham turned to Durk.

"So why are we here?" he asked. "What have you got that couldn't be discussed over the phone?"

"Frank has a story for you," Durk said. "And it's a doozy."

Burnham took a sip of coffee and nodded toward Frank. "I'm all yours."

With that, Frank spilled everything: the pad, the corruption, and the payoffs. When he finished, he looked at Burnham, waiting for a response.

"I'm not surprised," Burnham said, nodding. "The entire system is corrupt. I'll bet every business in the city is paying off the cops. Even the *Times* does. That's why our delivery trucks don't get ticketed when they're illegally parked."

"Jesus Christ," Frank said. "Even you guys are bribing the cops? Why the hell aren't you writing about it?"

Burnham shook his head. "My circulation editor told me to leave it alone. If he can't pay the cops, he'll never get the paper out on time."

The three men went silent for a moment, but Frank couldn't let it rest.

"Well, if you won't touch it, what's next?" he said. "I sent word to John Walsh and got nowhere. And the Department of Investigation wouldn't do anything, either. There's nobody left."

"Frank's right," Durk said to Burnham. "An article in the *Times* would definitely get Lindsay's attention. No mayor could ignore it; he'd have to do something."

Burnham palmed the sweat off his neck.

"Even if I can sell this to my editor," he said, "I'll need other sources besides you two. I'll need more cops to go on the record. No offense, Frank, but my editor will want to hear from a cop who's up the chain, somebody with a higher rank."

There was only one person Frank knew he could turn to: his partner, Paul Delise. And so, one night when he was off duty, Frank drove to Delise's house in the suburbs of Westchester County, north of the Bronx. When he arrived, Delise and his family were finishing dinner.

Delise invited Frank into the living room, where they could speak privately. Sitting in an armchair, Frank leaned forward and kept his voice low. In a near whisper, he told Delise about his meeting with Burnham.

"We need somebody higher up the ladder," he said. "We're just a couple of flunkies. The *Times* won't believe us, and even if they do, the public won't."

Frank didn't come right out with his question: Will *you* come with us to the *Times*? Delise had already done so much for him; Frank couldn't bring himself to put the guy on the spot again. But it didn't matter. He'd come here for a favor, and he didn't have to say it to be heard.

Delise stayed quiet, letting the silence hang in the air. Then he got up and poured a splash of whiskey into each of two glasses.

"Frank, I hear what you're saying," he said, handing Frank a glass.

"And, of course, I agree with you. I've seen the corruption for myself. But . . ." Delise stopped speaking. He shook his head and sipped his drink. "Are we really going to change anything? Because I've got a lot at risk. A house, a mortgage, my wife, six kids."

The guy had a legitimate concern. If the story blew up in his face, he could lose his livelihood, his house, everything. And if that happened, he'd have to answer to his family. Frank didn't have those kinds of responsibilities.

"I understand," Frank said, putting down his glass.

Delise looked at Frank, apologetically. "Police work is all I know. And it pays my bills."

"I get it," Frank said. "And I want to make it clear that I appreciate all you've done for me already." He got up to shake Delise's hand.

"No, no, stay," Delise said, nodding toward the chair.

Frank settled back in his seat, his face heating up from the embarrassment of being rejected by the one policeman he respected.

Delise downed the rest of his whiskey and stabbed his finger in the air. "Do what you have to do," he said. "And I'll back you one hundred percent."

"Are you sure?" Frank said.

"I'm sure. You're doing the right thing, for Chrissakes. I'm not going to send you in there alone."

Frank exhaled a great gust of air. This was what he'd been waiting to hear from so many others. Finally, somebody was in his corner—an inspector, no less.

"Thanks, Paul. I'm not sure how to thank you."

"You can start by staying alive. If this thing gets published, you're going to have every cop in the city gunning for you like never before."

On February 12, 1970, Frank sat nervously in a conference room in the *New York Times* building on West 43rd Street. David Burnham had arranged for his editor, Arthur Gelb, to meet with Frank and Durk. With Paul Delise once again by his side, Frank was confident his story would be taken seriously.

"Just because it sounds crazy doesn't mean it is," Frank said.

"So what you're telling me is that some cops in your division are crooked?" Gelb said, looking at Frank through a pair of tortoise-shell glasses.

Frank wasn't about to be intimidated by the powerful metro-politan editor. "No, no," he said. "This is about the whole damned department."

Burnham jumped in, backing up Frank. "This isn't the story of one or two cops who take money; this is a cancer in the department."

"Let's all calm down," Gelb said, standing up and pacing the room, his six-two frame adding to his imposing presence. "Tell me again about the pad. Start from the beginning. How does it work? Who gets paid? How much money are we talking? How many cops are involved?"

Frank started again from the top. He told them about the pay-offs, the envelope from Jewish Max, Stanard, Zumatto, the works. As he spoke, the room got quieter and quieter. Soon, the only sounds in the room were Frank's voice and the scratching sound of pen on paper as Burnham took notes.

When Frank finally stopped speaking, Gelb and Burnham looked at Delise.

"You can confirm these stories?" Gelb asked.

"Absolutely," Delise said. "Every word is true. I've seen it myself."

Gelb leaned his palms on the conference room table. "We'll need time to do our own investigating. If the story is about the entire force, we'll need more people in the department to go on the record."

By the time the meeting ended, it was nearly two in the morning. Gelb seemed convinced, and judging by the tone of his voice, it looked as though he was ready to bring the story to his boss, Managing Editor A. M. Rosenthal.

Arthur Gelb (left) works alongside A. M. "Abe" Rosenthal at the New York Times.

Frank got into the elevator with Durk and Delise. Minutes later, when they stepped outside, he barely noticed a blast of frigid air. All he knew was that he hadn't felt this hopeful in years.

"Well?" Durk asked, wrapping his navy wool scarf around his neck. "What'd you think?"

"It's not what I think," Frank said. "It's what they think. Burnham gets it. Gelb, I'm pretty sure, does, too. It looks good, but we'll find out soon enough."

Then, before heading toward 7th Avenue, Frank turned to Delise and reached out his gloved hand. "If it weren't for you, we'd be back at square one."

"Well, they have the story now," Delise said, shaking Frank's hand. "Let's hope they don't leave anything out."

Frank headed home on his motorcycle, all the while replaying the meeting in his head. Each time he did, he came away with the same thought: If the *Times* would print the story, he'd blow the whole damned system apart, once and for all.

– I Remember Paul Delise –

Even now, I get choked up thinking about Paul Delise. There he was, an inspector, partnering with me, a two-bit cop. Can you imagine? We were on rooftops, in alleys, inside basements catching crooks. It must have been tough for a guy his age. Still, I think he had some fun. It was good, old-fashioned policework, just the two of us out there risking our necks.

The other cops couldn't stand it—they used to tail us when we left the station house, making sure we didn't step on their turf and ruin business. That gives you an idea of just how rotten things had become.

The night I went to Delise's house, the night he told me he'd back me up, was a life-changing moment. It shouldn't have been that way. It shouldn't have been so hard to find one respectable guy on the force.

But when you're the only one fighting for justice, you become the enemy. And Delise knew that. By backing me up, he must've lost a lot of friends in the department, and by the way, he probably put his own life on the line.

I'll never know why he stuck his neck out for me. I guess we just both believed the system was broken, and we were the ones who could fix it.

I can't speak for everybody, but I'm betting all of us—the outsiders, the misfits, the so-called freaks—remember the person who stood up for us. We remember the guy who shouts, "Dammit, he's my friend, and he's right, and you're wrong."

And so, I remember Paul Delise. He was there when I needed him most. He's no longer with us, but I'm sure he's in good company with all the other saints.

But don't get me wrong. Just because he was willing to go on the record doesn't mean the rest of the police force suddenly found religion. Far from it.

Chapter Five

FRANK WENT BACK TO MANHATTAN NORTH AND WORKED HIS territory, tracking and arresting gambling operators. In the process, he waited for the *Times* to publish the story. Two months went by and nothing happened. He knew the paper was doing its own investigating, but he was beginning to put the *Times* on his list of dead-end leads.

Then, on Friday, April 24, 1970, he was sitting in the back of an unmarked patrol car. Two plainclothesmen sat in the front.

The driver caught Frank's eye in the rearview mirror. "So, I hear you went before the grand jury and you didn't hold back."

"Really?" Frank said, trying his best to keep a poker face. "Where'd you hear that?

"We have our informants."

"Wow, that's pretty good. I wish I had informants like that," Frank said, looking out the window, keeping his eyes off the cop. There was no telling what these guys knew. Why risk letting them read his face?

The cop kept on talking. "Well, you'll read about it tomorrow. It's coming out in the *Times*."

Frank was dumbfounded. Was the story finally being printed? And if it was, how did these guys know about it?

Again, the cop eyed Frank through the rearview mirror. "Gee, who do you think could've blabbed to the *Times*? I sure hope whoever opened his big mouth had the good sense not to give names. Know what I mean, Serpico? A guy like that could find himself dead in an alley somewhere. It's dangerous out there."

"Yep, I hear you," Frank said. "But if you're clean, you've got nothing to worry about."

As soon as his shift ended, Frank ran to a pay phone and called Burnham.

"The article is running tomorrow?" Frank said. "Why the hell didn't you tell me? I had to find out from cops in my unit."

"I've been trying to reach you," Burnham said. "It'll be out tomorrow. Front page."

At four thirty the next morning, as the sun was coming up, Frank stood at the Sheridan Square newsstand, his heart pounding furiously as he handed the vendor a dime. Then he slid a copy of the *Times* from the stack of papers piled in front of him. There it was, in the upper left corner of the front page:

GRAFT PAID TO POLICE HERE
SAID TO RUN INTO MILLIONS

Frank's story makes the front page, April 25, 1970.

The article continues on page 18, sparing no officials from scrutiny.

Finally.

Frank's story was no longer the stuff of secret meetings on dark street corners. After years of broken promises and false leads, the truth was out in the open, about to be read by a million people—including every New York City bigwig from Lindsay to Walsh. No matter what happened to Frank, the story now had a life of its own.

And it was obvious Burnham hadn't pulled any punches.

"Narcotics dealers, gamblers and businessmen," he wrote, "make illicit payments of millions of dollars a year to the policemen of New York, according to policemen, law-enforcement experts and New Yorkers who make such payments themselves."

Burnham didn't mention Frank, Durk, or Delise by name. Instead, he wrote, "The names of the policemen who discussed corruption with The Times are being withheld to protect them from possible reprisals."

The more Frank read, the more he realized how much investigating the *Times* had done on its own. Burnham let it be known that he had spoken to "several commanding officers" and that they had agreed to "talk to The Times about the problem of corruption because, they charged, city officials had been remiss in investigating corruption."

The article went on to say, "The policemen and private citizens who talked to The Times describe a situation in which payoffs by gamblers to policemen are almost commonplace, in which some policemen accept bribes from narcotics dealers, in which businessmen throughout the city are subjected to extortion to cover up infractions of law and in which internal payoffs among policemen seem to have become institutionalized."

The *Times* identified Philip Foran, Cornelius Behan, and Arnold Fraiman as three of the police officials who had failed to investigate the charges when given a chance.

Frank turned to page 18, where the rest of the story took up nearly the entire broadsheet. Burnham had laid out story after story of corruption throughout the department. He even mentioned the envelope from Jewish Max, quoting "a policeman" who said Captain Foran told him that if he chose to blab, he'd wind up "floating in the East River, face down."

This was Frank's story translated into newspaper ink.

The *Times* article was too big to ignore. In fact, it was so big that it spread like a virus clear across the globe. Newspapers from San Francisco to London picked up the story, highlighting system-wide corruption that ran into the tens of millions of dollars.

Over the next few days, the *Times* ran two more page-one stories on police corruption, both by Burnham. One detailed how plain-clothes officers decided which gambling bosses to put on their payroll and how much to charge them. The other revealed how the corruption affected morale. How could an honest cop feel good about going to work if the job wasn't on the level?

Almost immediately, Police Commissioner Howard Leary reacted with fury, accusing the *Times* of going too far by painting all cops as corrupt. "Just to take a brush and sweep everyone under that brush," he said, "is unfair."

For his part, Mayor Lindsay launched into damage control. He wanted the public to believe he'd known about the corruption and had the problem well in hand. He issued an official statement that read, in part, "Police Commissioner Leary has advised me that many of the allegations in this story came from one particular patrolman and were reported to the department in 1967 . . . The department investigated these allegations, referred them to the Bronx district attorney's office and, as a result, a number of indictments were handed down."

But the topic became such a lightning rod that Lindsay soon reversed course. He called the charges "extremely serious" and promised that the allegations would be investigated immediately.

Soon after, Commissioner Leary released a statement to be read in all police precincts throughout the city. In it, he urged any cop with firsthand knowledge of corruption to speak up.

If they did, he promised, there would be no retaliation against them.

Nobody in blue believed him.

In June 1970, a reluctant Frank was sitting in the witness box in the Bronx Supreme Court. It had been two months since the story broke in the *Times* and nearly a year and a half since the grand jury had issued its indictments.

Stanard was now on trial for perjury—that is, he was charged with lying to the grand jury when he said he wasn't on the pad at the 7th Division.

Before testifying, Frank got a mouthful from Bronx DA Burton Roberts. This time it was over Frank's appearance.

"Goddammit, Serpico, cut your hair," Roberts screamed at him. "You're a crucial witness. Try to look presentable for a change."

"Why?" Frank said. "I'm not the one on trial."

Frank thought better of it and agreed to shave his beard—but left a long handlebar mustache. It was a message of defiance, a reminder to Roberts that he never wanted to be there in the first place. But at this point, there was no turning back—and no calming Frank's nerves. Here he was, dressed in a conservative gray suit, about to ID a fellow cop.

Then he looked at Stanard sitting at the defense table and became convinced he was doing the right thing. He felt no pity for Stanard. No pangs of guilt. No anything. The guy was no longer a cop. In fact, he had never been a policeman, not in the true sense of the word. The guy was just another two-bit criminal.

And so, when prompted by Roberts, Frank recounted, step by step, how gambling bosses had lined the pockets of Stanard and the rest of his cronies in the 7th Division.

"The gamblers paid the cops up to eight hundred dollars a month," he said, dragging his fingers over his mustache. "The boys carried the cash in a satchel and split it amongst the group. I saw it all. I've even heard cops haggle with gamblers over money, negotiating rates and other charges. And Stanard was in on all of it."

Frank also testified that he'd first reported widespread corruption in 1967, soon after being transferred to the 7th Division.

After Frank finished, Roberts called Dolores Carreras's husband, Juan, to the stand, and asked him to explain how the pad worked.

"Zumatto said there was a $2,000 initiation," Juan Carreras said.

"And $800 a month—not including the lieutenants and up—for the division and $150 for the precinct."

Carreras kept on going. There was another five hundred a month for the plainclothes squad and two hundred for the detectives. He also testified that Stanard had brought in a gambling boss, Ricardo Ramos from Jersey City, to help bankroll the racket.

Stanard denied all of it. But the jury didn't believe him.

On June 30, twelve days after his perjury trial began, Stanard was found guilty. He would be sentenced to one-to-three years in a state penitentiary. Zumatto and Paretti would eventually cop a plea, ducking prison time. But all three would be off the force for good.

Still, Frank wasn't happy. What good was getting rid of those guys? Unless somebody fixed the whole rotten system, there'd be new Stanards to fill their shoes. Worse yet, most of the other cops in the city didn't blame Stanard, Zumatto, and Paretti for being crooked. They blamed Frank for exposing them.

Frank leaves the Bronx courthouse after testifying on police corruption.

After Stanard's trial, Frank got word that the Bronx DA had sent a letter to Commissioner Leary. Roberts felt that the department should reward Frank for his efforts in exposing corruption by promoting him to detective. Roberts told Leary how Frank had testified before the grand jury and then again at Stanard's perjury trial. He said Frank had shown moral courage when he stuck his neck out without any ulterior motives. Besides, he said, Frank had just been transferred to narcotics in Brooklyn South. He was working in the detective division anyway. He just didn't have the rank to go with the assignment.

Leary, apparently, didn't see Frank the same way. "He's a psycho," he told Roberts.

"In that case, perhaps the department needs more psychos," Roberts said. "Seriously, I really think he should get it."

"Not while I'm police commissioner."

Leary's decision was final.

But there was no putting out the fire that Frank had started. The *Times* had focused so much attention on the police that Lindsay announced the formation of a special five-person commission to investigate charges of corruption in the department. He appointed New York attorney Whitman Knapp to lead the Commission to Investigate Allegations of Police Corruption and the City's Anti-Corruption Procedures, which quickly became known as the Knapp Commission.

The pressure proved to be too much for Leary. On September 5, four months after the *Times*'s blockbuster revelations, the mayor announced Leary's resignation. In Frank's words, he "got the hell out of Dodge."

Leary's replacement, Patrick Murphy, who had once served on the force, was hired to clean up Leary's mess.

Meanwhile, Frank was getting a fresh start in Brooklyn South, investigating narcotics-related crimes. This was a new assignment and a new command that covered sixteen precincts and nearly two million residents. Frank didn't know it yet, but Brooklyn South was just as dirty as the 7th Division in the Bronx. The only difference was that instead of stealing from gambling bosses, the cops in Brooklyn were stealing from drug dealers.

On one of his first outings, Frank was walking his beat when a car pulled up alongside him. A sergeant was behind the wheel.

The sarge called to Frank out of his open window. "Hey, you're Serpico, right?"

"Yeah."

"Get in. I want to talk with you."

"Sure," Frank said, sliding into the passenger seat.

"You wired?" the sarge asked him.

What the hell was this? He'd just started on the job, and he was already being hassled. "No," he said. "I don't walk the streets wearing a goddamned wire."

"Good, because this conversation isn't for anyone else's ears."

"Yeah, okay. What do you want?"

"You're in Brooklyn now," the sarge said as he put the car in gear and began to drive. "This isn't the Bronx. This is the real deal."

"Yeah, so?"

"So we have drugs here. Heroin. It's no joyride; I'm talking gangs and guns. But the payoff is huge, totally worth it, not the nickel-and-dime stuff you guys were dealing with up there."

"What are you saying?" Frank said.

"Do you want in on the action?"

Was this guy kidding? Didn't he read the papers? Frank had just testified against cops for taking money from gambling bosses. Why would he join in with these brutes? They were leaving drugs on the street, helping heroin dealers tear apart hardworking families.

"No, thanks," Frank said. "You do what you do. I don't take money."

The sarge gave him a puzzled look. "You sure you're not wired?"

"Yeah, I'm sure. And you can let me out here."

"Okay, but don't screw around. Do I make myself clear?"

Actually, he couldn't have been clearer: Frank was an outsider. Again.

And these guys in narcotics were obviously a lot different from those in gambling. These weren't grass eaters—small-time cops skimming gambling money—they were savage, bloodthirsty meat eaters.

If Frank had to, he'd bring them down, too.

Assuming they didn't get to him first.

The Michael Dowd Drug Ring

Michael Dowd is disgraced on the front page of the New York Daily News, *September 28, 1993.*

One of the most notorious corruption scandals in the history of the NYPD broke in 1992, when cocaine was ravaging many communities. At the center of the storm was Michael Dowd, a patrolman in Brooklyn.

While in uniform, Dowd and a ring of dirty cops ran a criminal enterprise that involved buying and selling cocaine, stealing money from drug dealers, and tipping off dealers about police raids. Dowd was pocketing so much money—as much as several thousand dollars a week—that he sometimes forgot to collect his paycheck. After a decade on the force, he was convicted of racketeering and conspiracy to distribute cocaine. He served twelve years in prison.

The scandal led Mayor David Dinkins to establish a commission, headed by retired judge Milton Mollen, to look into wrongdoing in the NYPD, the sixth such investigation since the formation of the department. The commission found that police officials had failed to look into reports of corruption and that senior officers had ignored the situation to protect their own careers.

In the wake of the report, the New York City Council proposed the creation of an outside agency to investigate police misconduct. Dinkins's successor, Rudolph Giuliani, vetoed the proposal, insisting that the police department did not need outside intervention to uphold its integrity.

– A Lesson from My Mother –

As you can imagine, the stress of going to work was killing me. I was alone. I had no friends on the force. I was desperate.

I suppose everybody finds inner strength somewhere, and I kept finding mine in the lessons my parents had taught me. I can still remember a parable my mother told me when we went shopping one day. The story goes that a woman took her young son to a sewing shop, and when they got home, he reached into his pocket and took out a bunch of sewing needles he'd swiped from the store. His mother patted him on the back and told him he was a "good boy."

In time, the boy got into the habit of stealing more and more, and when he was older, he got into so much trouble that he landed on death row. Before his execution, he asked to see his mother. So she came to the prison and stood outside his cell.

He said, "Come closer, Mother."

She pressed her face against the bars, expecting a kiss. Instead, he bit her hard on the nose and said, "If you would've pricked my finger with one of those needles, I wouldn't be in here now."

Yeah, I know. It's a corny story. But my mother's point was clear: There's a right way to live your life, and there's a wrong way.

So what was I supposed to do with the boys in narcotics? Let them continue taking money from drug dealers? Leave those drugs on the street?

What would my mother have thought if I walked away?

Chapter Six

On a bitter cold Wednesday, February 3, 1971, Frank spent the morning taking care of his usual chores. He cleaned his apartment, dropped his dirty clothes off at the laundromat, and shopped for groceries. Afterward, he went to the police academy firing range, where he took extra target practice with each of his three guns: his service weapon, the Browning semiautomatic, and his Smith & Wesson .38 snub-nose revolver.

Late in the afternoon, he got a call from a Brooklyn North team leader, Gary Roteman.

"I got some information from a CI," Roteman said, referring to a confidential informant who worked for him. "Get your butt over here. We could pick up a few arrests tonight."

Frank grabbed his guns and went to Brooklyn North Narcotics at the 94th Precinct in the neighborhood of Greenpoint. There, he met up with the three cops whom he'd never met but who would be his partners that night: Roteman, Arthur Cesare, and Paul Halley. All three were plainclothes, but it was hard to believe they thought they could blend in with the locals. Even a casual glance at their dark overcoats, leather shoes, and neatly trimmed haircuts could blow an operation.

Roteman was lean with graying hair. Cesare had dark skin and a straight nose. Halley had a pale, round face with tiny eyes. Those faces could have been obscured had they grown big, bushy beards, as Frank did. Instead, these three made no attempt at hiding their identities.

"My CI's waiting at his apartment," Roteman told them as they piled into an unmarked car.

When they arrived at the address in nearby Williamsburg, they picked up the informant, a young Puerto Rican man with gold-framed glasses.

"I thought you guys would never get here," he said, rubbing his hands together in the freezing cold as they walked to the car.

"Well, we're here now," Cesare said. "Get in."

The CI climbed into the back seat and told them to head to Driggs Avenue.

"What number?" Roteman asked.

"778. Turn onto Driggs and I'll stop you when you get to the building."

Within minutes, they drove past the run-down, six-story apartment house. Judging by its ornate façade, the place might have been fancy in its day, but that day was long gone.

778 Driggs Avenue in Brooklyn

"A dealer named Mambo lives on the third floor," the CI said. "He's pushing heroin."

"We'll find out soon enough," Roteman said, circling the block and then coming back to Driggs, this time parking next to a deserted schoolyard halfway up the block.

The four cops hatched a plan. The CI knew the junkies in the neighborhood, so he would hang out on the street and keep an eye on the building to see who went in and out. If he thought somebody was there to do business with Mambo, he'd wipe his glasses with his handkerchief. That would signal to the cops that the person was carrying heroin.

At eight o'clock, the CI took his position at the building's entrance. It was dark out, but a nearby streetlamp threw some light on the front door, which the cops were watching through a pair of binoculars.

An hour went by. Then when a woman walked out of the building holding a shopping bag, the informant removed his glasses and wiped them. Roteman, Cesare, and Halley got out of the car and trailed her. A few minutes later, the three cops returned, having searched the woman and come up empty.

Another hour passed and no suspects left the building. Roteman suggested that Frank go inside and see what he could find.

"Why me?" Frank asked, but he knew the answer. He was the only one in the car who didn't look like a cop. Besides his bushy beard, he sported jeans and calf-high boots, along with a turtleneck sweater and a leather vest under a padded army jacket.

He got out of the car and strode across the street, carrying his service revolver in an old gas-mask bag slung over his shoulder like a knapsack.

When he got to the building, he didn't acknowledge the CI. Instead, he walked straight inside, stepping over the garbage that cluttered the foyer. The place was seedy, to say the least. Dirt covered the floor, and the stink of urine filled the hallways.

As he climbed the stairs, he instinctively checked for his other two weapons. His Browning was tucked into a belt holster on his left hip. The snub-nose was holstered in his belt on the right side, but he wanted it closer, so he took it out and put it in his jacket pocket.

He continued climbing, one flight, then another, and another. Staticky music spilled out from behind doors, and the odors from people's apartments leaked into the air. Frying pork. Beef broth. Marijuana. When he reached the top landing, he tiptoed around a sleeping, unwashed mutt, side-stepping clumps of dog shit, and made his way onto the roof. In the distance, the lights of the Williamsburg Bridge twinkled in the darkened sky.

Torn glassine bags and old tubes of model-airplane glue littered the ground. These were sure signs of drug use. The bags were the kind used by dealers to package small amounts of heroin, and the glue was the kind inhaled by junkies for a cheap, desperate buzz. Mambo's customers must've been coming up here to get high.

"Pssst."

The voice came from the rooftop doorway. Frank reached for his Browning, then relaxed when he saw the CI standing on the landing.

"Mambo's in 3G," the CI said. "Things are heating up."

"Okay. Go back downstairs and watch the entrance."

When the CI left, Frank peered over the roofline, waiting for him to reappear at his post. In the glow of the streetlamp, he saw two guys heading into the building. He ran back inside and tiptoed down the steps, stopping before the third floor, listening to their patter as they shuffled up the stairs.

Sure enough, they stopped at 3G.

Frank looked down the stairway. One of the guys knocked on the red apartment door and mumbled a few words. The door opened a crack—it was guarded by a short security chain—and the guy handed some cash to the person inside. That must be Mambo. The door shut, but it soon reopened when Mambo slipped them a glassine envelope. The door shut again, this time for good. The deal was done.

Frank tailed the men out of the building, keeping his distance; when he reached the street, he motioned to Roteman, Cesare, and Halley.

The cops jumped out of the car and stopped the buyers. Frisking them, they found two bags of heroin in their pockets. That clinched it. Now there was no doubt about what was going on in Mambo's apartment. They handcuffed the suspects and put them in the back of the police car. Halley got in the driver's seat and drove off to book them at the station house, leaving Roteman, Cesare, and Frank behind.

Roteman came up with a plan: Frank would go directly to Mambo's apartment and make a buy. That is, he'd pretend he was a junkie looking to score some heroin.

"Me again?" Frank said.

"You're the only one of us who speaks Spanish," Roteman said.

"Okay, but then what?"

"Just get Mambo to open the door. And leave the rest to me and Cesare."

Seconds later, the three cops were inside the building, climbing the stairs to apartment 3G. The red door was just to the right of the landing. Cesare positioned himself on the stairway between the second and third floors. Roteman pressed his body against the door of the neighboring apartment to keep out of sight.

Slipping his right hand into his army jacket pocket, Frank took out his .38 snub-nose and held it low, alongside his leg. Then, with his left hand, he knocked on the door, put his face in front of the peephole, and said in Spanish that a guy named Joe had sent him and that he needed something.

"Joe me mandó. Necesito algo."

The minute the door opened, Frank pushed his body against it, snapping the security chain. He raised his gun, but Mambo pushed back. Frank's body was pinned in the doorway, but he managed to point his revolver at Mambo.

It was a standoff between the two, each one pushing on either side of the door, while Roteman and Cesare stood motionless.

Frank snapped his head around to see where they were. "What the hell are you guys waiting for?" he yelled. When he turned back to look at Mambo, he was hit with a burst of light, as if somebody had tossed a lit firecracker in his face.

The bullet tore through his left cheek, just below his eye.

As he staggered to the floor, he fired back, hitting Mambo, who screamed and ran back into the apartment.

Lying on his back, in shock and fear, Frank looked up at the ceiling, his left eye swollen shut, his vision blurred, and a gush of warm blood rolling down his face. Cesare was bent over him, silent.

"For God's sake," Frank muttered, barely able to speak. "Stop the bleeding. Use my scarf. Do something."

Roteman's voice rang out from inside the apartment. "Police! Drop the guns and come out with your hands up."

The hallway faded in and out as Frank battled to stay conscious, afraid he'd drift off to sleep and never again open his eyes.

The action continued to play out around him.

Roteman burst out of the apartment and bolted down the stairs, and Cesare gave chase behind him. They were no doubt hunting Mambo, who must have fled out the fire escape. But whatever they were doing, they'd left Frank alone, dying.

Just then, an elderly man came out of a nearby apartment, shuffled over to Frank, and knelt by his side.

"Don't worry," the man said in a soft Spanish accent. "You'll be all right. I called the police."

Minutes later, a siren wailed in the distance, and then footsteps bounded up the stairs. Frank could barely make out the two uniformed cops who picked him up, carried him out to the street, and slid him into the back seat of their patrol car—but he did recognize the look of panic on their faces. And, as he lay in the back of the car, speeding to Greenpoint Hospital, he was all too familiar with the sound of the siren. He just couldn't believe it was for him.

The scene came in flashes, in bursts of visuals. The gurney. The beeline past the emergency room. The nurses peeling off his jacket, his sweater, his boots. The blood. The needles going into his arms.

"He's a cop," somebody said.

"Bullet hole. Right here. Left cheek, above the nostril."

Frank tried to get the attention of a uniformed cop in the room, but he couldn't turn his head. Or move his lips.

"Don't call my mother," he tried to spit out. He hoped to save her from seeing her son bleed out in a room filled with cops who'd probably celebrate his final breath. "Call my sister. Call my sister."

Frank had no idea if anybody heard him. All he could do was lie there, helpless, as a priest stood over him, administering last rites— the final prayer uttered before a Catholic person dies.

Chapter Seven

THE MORNING AFTER THE SHOOTING, FRANK LAY ON HIS BACK in a ward on the third floor of Greenpoint Hospital, staring at the ceiling, which loomed two stories overhead.

He couldn't be dead, because he was able to make out the cracked white plaster and hear the commotion around him. Nurses shuttled in and out of the huge room, wheeling trays of medications to the half-dozen other patients in the room. Police officers stood by the door nearest to Frank's bed, muttering his name, probably wishing the cop car that saved him had gotten stuck in traffic.

A doctor stopped at Frank's bedside and spoke quietly. Frank could hear out of only one ear and tried his best to focus. His left eye was swollen shut and he struggled to breathe; a bandage covered half his face and rubber tubes dangled from his chest. Still, he got the basic story: The bullet, a .22-caliber, had entered his cheek just below his left eye and shattered into fragments. The ER surgeon was able to remove all of the pieces except one, which sat so close to Frank's brain, it hadn't seemed worth the risk to dislodge it.

"You're a lucky guy," the doctor said. "That bullet came within an eyelash of your brain. But, in this case, an eyelash might as well be a mile."

It looked as though Frank was out of immediate danger. Still, Mambo's bullet had done its damage. According to the doctors, he would never again hear out of his left ear. It was tough news to take. Opera music, which he loved so dearly, would now sound different, as would rustling leaves and his friends' voices. But it beat dying.

From what Frank had put together, things hadn't gone much better for Mambo, who'd been brought to the same hospital shortly after Frank was wheeled in. Mambo was in the surgical ward, one floor above Frank, nursing two gunshot wounds: one in his wrist, where he'd caught Frank's bullet, and another in his stomach, courtesy of the narcotics cop who had cornered him trying to sneak out of an apartment a half mile from 778 Driggs.

"You're looking fine, young fella." The voice belonged to Police Commissioner Patrick Murphy, who was standing by Frank's bed, along with Mayor Lindsay. "Are you getting everything you need?"

A list of answers popped into Frank's head, all of which were bitter, sarcastic, and fueled with rage. But spitting them out would have taken too much effort.

"I'm okay," Frank muttered.

Murphy and Lindsay said all the usual meaningless bullcrap that people say in hospitals—we're pulling for you, Frank, hang in there, kid—but neither of them asked the questions that were plaguing Frank: Had he been set up? Did Roteman and Cesare send him to apartment 3G hoping he'd get shot? If not, why did they disappear? Why had they left him there to die?

Mayor Lindsay faced a throng of reporters outside the hospital, updating the media on Frank's condition.

"He's a brave man," Lindsay said, referring to Frank's participation in the buy-and-bust sting at Mambo's apartment. "And he deserves the highest praise."

What Lindsay didn't mention was Frank's more heroic battle—the one against corruption, dishonesty, and the police force itself.

Twenty-four hours later, Frank found himself in the relative comfort of a private facility, Brooklyn Jewish Hospital, where he was tended to by a team of neurosurgeons. There he was fed intravenously and kept in a darkened room. A hospital spokesperson reported that Frank was in "fair" condition but was not receiving any visitors.

Frank was leaning on his pillow, groggy from the antibiotics and unsure of what handicaps he'd have for the rest of his life, when a figure approached his bed. It was Arthur Cesare.

Frank gritted his teeth and spat out his words in a hoarse whisper. "Why don't you go back to the academy and learn how to shoot?"

"Screw you," Cesare said, holding an envelope. "I came to give you this. It's your watch. I found it on the floor of the building."

"Maybe you should get a medal for that," Frank said, not bothering to ask why Cesare hadn't backed him up. "Get out."

Cesare put the watch on Frank's bed and left without saying another word.

As time went on, Frank regained his strength. The swelling in his face had begun to go down, although he ran into one setback after another. First, he developed a fever. Then the veins in his left leg swelled, putting him in a wheelchair and eventually leaving him with a limp.

Get well cards arrived in the mail, along with greetings from cops who Frank knew did not want to see him recuperate.

One such card, sent anonymously, came with a handwritten message. Under the printed phrase "with sincere sympathy," the sender had scrawled "that you didn't get your brains blown out, you rat bastard. Happy relapse."

After six weeks, Frank was finally fit enough to leave the hospital. A fellow officer drove him in an unmarked car to the Brooklyn

North command. There he picked up his belongings, his guns, and a cardboard box filled with his clothes, which had been sitting untouched since the night of the shooting.

When he walked into his apartment on Perry Street, he opened the box and found a plastic bag filled with his bloodstained clothes. He ripped open the bag, pulled out his boots, and tossed the clothes in the trash.

In a perfect world, everything would have returned to normal. But Frank was now deaf in his left ear, and with his left leg dragging, he'd become dependent on a cane. And he had frequent skull-splitting headaches.

His career as a crimefighter was over. He spent his days sitting on a Hudson River pier with his sheepdog, Alfie, gazing out at the water.

A month after the shooting, department officials questioned Roteman and Cesare to understand how a cop could be shot and left by his partners to die.

Roteman said that one of the shots coming from inside Mambo's apartment had whizzed by him on the landing.

"We were in a state of shock," he said.

After help arrived, Roteman said, he and Cesare "ordered the occupants to come out with their hands up."

The story might have made sense, except that it contradicted everything Roteman had said in the early morning hours after the shooting. Back then, Roteman said he'd seen the flash of gunfire from inside Mambo's apartment, had fired two shots in return, and told Cesare to run into a neighboring apartment and call for help.

Cesare also had some memory lapses when explaining his own actions. "I fired one shot into the apartment as two of the perpetrators were going out the back window down the fire escape," he said. "I then ran down the stairs to make a notification for an ambulance and assistance."

His story didn't match the one Roteman had given. Nor did it match the explanation he himself had given after the shooting. At the time, he said he was trying to pull Frank out of the apartment, but when the shot rang out, he pushed Frank inside.

Even more curious was that the radio signal Cesare and Roteman sent out was a 10-10, police code for shots fired between two unknown people. The situation called for a 10-13. That's the signal given when an officer has been shot or needs help, the one that was appropriate, the one that would have brought an army of cops. Instead, precious time was lost as Frank lay on the floor, dying.

Had it not been for the neighbor who'd called for the ambulance, that distinction—the broadcasting of a 10-10 instead of a 10-13—could have been the difference between life and death.

After questioning Roteman and Cesare, the department determined that they had acted courageously and awarded each a medal of exceptional merit for saving Frank's life. It also gave a medal to Maxwell Katz, the patrolman who captured Edgar Echevarria, the drug dealer known on the street as Mambo.

On May 3, 1971, three months after the shooting, Frank was on the cover of *New York* magazine. More specifically, his skull was on the cover. The magazine printed an X-ray of Frank's head, complete with a graphic bull's-eye indicating the location of the .22-caliber bullet that was lodged near his brain. The headline read, "Portrait of an Honest Cop: Target for Attack."

The eight-page article detailed Frank's journey—his frustration with the corruption around him and his attempts to alert his superiors—and ended by saying he could no longer continue his quest.

The article also quoted a high-ranking police official who said, "When word came in that Serpico had been shot, this building shook. We were terrified that a cop had done it."

That official wasn't alone. It seemed that journalists, police officers, even the public, felt that Frank had been set up. Frank wasn't convinced, although he did have a lot of questions about why his partners had left him lying in that hallway, bleeding, a step from death.

Meanwhile, the Knapp Commission that Mayor Lindsay created was more than a year into its investigation. The Patrolmen's Benevolent Association, the union representing police officers, had tried every move possible to block the inquiry. The association refused to cooperate. It filed a lawsuit. Its rank and file even went on strike for seven days.

But the commission survived. It conducted its first set of public hearings in October, and on Tuesday, December 14, 1971, was about to begin another session. The leadoff witness was none other than the man in the eye of the storm.

Frank, accompanied by his lawyer, former U.S. Attorney General Ramsey Clark, entered the Great Hall of the Chamber of Commerce Building in downtown Manhattan, navigating his way through a swarm of reporters.

A journalist called out to Clark, "Why does Serpico need a lawyer?"

"He doesn't," Clark said. "I'm here to make sure he can say what he wants to say without being interrupted."

Frank had dressed for the occasion. He'd chosen a dark suit, striped shirt, and silk tie; he'd also trimmed his beard and blow-dried his hair. And, paying homage to a proud cobbler, he'd stopped for a shoeshine on his way to the hearings. As Vincenzo Serpico always said, people assess you from the ground up.

Frank walked into the hall ready to tell his story. Making his way to his seat, he couldn't help but think that this whole circus could have been avoided if just one department official had been willing to fight the status quo. Just one.

Chapter Eight

FRANK SAT AT A TABLE COVERED IN MICROPHONES AND glanced around the cavernous room, at the news cameras, the radio crews, the popping flashbulbs. His face was no doubt filling television screens in living rooms across the city, and his statements would surely be read by millions more in tomorrow's papers.

Frank appears before the Knapp Commission, 1971.

In preparation for his appearance, which was broadcast in its entirety on New York City's public television station, Frank had met with Michael Armstrong, the commission's chief counsel. Armstrong had spent more than a year investigating Frank's charges, making sure his version of events could be corroborated. It was during one of their conversations that Frank laid out for Armstrong how he saw the state of police corruption.

"Ten percent of the cops in New York City are absolutely corrupt," he had said, "ten percent are absolutely honest, and the other eighty percent wish they were honest."

Armstrong, who sported a thick mane of dark hair and long sideburns, leaned into the microphone in front of him and prompted Frank with questions.

"Mr. Serpico, can you tell us when you became a police officer?"

Frank told his story, providing a blow-by-blow account of his career in uniform. He told the commission how in 1959 he'd started as a wide-eyed rookie at Brooklyn's 81st Precinct, only to bounce through various assignments—the Bureau of Criminal Identification, Brooklyn's 90th Precinct, the Bronx's 7th Division, and Manhattan North—before landing back in Brooklyn in narcotics.

Frank spoke of the corruption he'd seen, explaining how the pad worked, how much money was involved, and how every cop took part. He even talked about the envelope from Jewish Max and how he had told his superiors about the $300 bribe.

With flashbulbs going off every other second, Frank told how he'd gone from one official to the next, alerting them to the corruption he'd seen. And he identified those officials by name.

Arnold Fraiman, the head of the Department of Investigation.

Jay Kriegel, chief of staff to Mayor Lindsay.

Philip Foran, the police captain who had warned him not to go before the grand jury unless he wanted to end up "floating in the East River, face down."

By the time he finished, three hours had gone by. Having delivered his testimony, he said he'd like to read a statement that he had prepared the night before.

The chairman of the commission, Whitman Knapp, looked at Frank over a pair of black horn-rimmed eyeglasses. "Please, go ahead."

Frank took out a sheet of paper and read in a calm, soft voice:

> Through my appearances here today I hope that police officers in the future will not experience the same frustration and anxiety that I was subjected to for the past five years at the hands of my superiors because of my attempt to report corruption . . .
>
> We must create an atmosphere in which the dishonest officer fears the honest one, and not the other way around. I hope that this investigation and any future ones will deal with corruption at all levels within the department and not limit themselves to cases involving individual patrolmen.
>
> Police corruption cannot exist unless it is at least tolerated at higher levels in the department. Therefore, the most important result that can come from these hearings is a conviction by police officers, even more than the public, that the department will change . . .
>
> Every patrolman is an officer and should be treated as such by his superiors. A policeman's attitude about himself reflects in large measure the attitude of his superiors toward him. If they feel his job is important and has stature, so will he.

When Frank finished, many in the room broke into applause. It felt as though a boulder had been lifted off his back.

He walked out of the Great Hall, knowing one thing for sure: Whatever lay ahead had to be better than this.

Modern-Day Whistleblowers

In 2021, *USA Today* published an investigation into police whistleblowers. The results were undeniable: Little has changed since Frank blew the whistle on police corruption in the 1970s. According to the *USA Today* story, the blue wall of silence still exists in police departments around the country. As the article states, "Police departments hunt down and silence internal whistleblowers to cover up misconduct with impunity."

It's not that legislators haven't tried to break the blue wall. Most states have enacted whistleblower laws to protect employees, including police officers, who report corruption and other wrongdoing.

Still, the stories persist.

In 2008, NYPD officer Adrian Schoolcraft began secretly recording his colleagues and superior officers manipulating crime statistics. A few weeks after reporting what he found to the Internal Affairs Bureau in October 2009, he was taken from his home and held against his will for six days in a psychiatric ward. He ultimately sued the NYPD, saying there was "a coordinated and concentrated effort" to silence him.

Baltimore police officer Joseph Crystal was harassed for two years after reporting the unjustified beating of a suspect in 2011. His fellow officers called him a rat, threatened his career, and pressured him into quitting his job and leaving the state.

In 2019, Sergeant Isaac Lambert was dropped from the Chicago Police Department's detective division down to patrol after he refused to lie on a police report detailing the shooting of an unarmed teenager. Lambert went on to sue the department for what he called an "act of retaliation."

> "I wanted every cop to know that you have to stand for something," he said. "That poor kid didn't deserve being shot for some bullshit, and the cop that did it doesn't deserve to be a cop."
>
> He also said, "I'm going to feel like Serpico."

Following Frank's appearance, the commission called high-ranking police officials to testify. It was their turn to respond to the charges Frank had levied against them.

Behan, who'd since been promoted to inspector, confirmed that Frank had contacted him, but said they'd never discussed specifics. Behan claimed he'd passed the information on to First Deputy Commissioner John Walsh, the man who built his reputation on cleaning up the force.

The commission asked Walsh himself why he hadn't acted on such a credible piece of evidence. Walsh responded that he'd "dropped the ball" and simply forgotten about the matter.

"I said I would meet with Serpico," Walsh said. "Unfortunately, that meeting never took place. I expected the meeting to be arranged by Inspector Behan. When it was not arranged, the incident left my mind."

Knapp, in an uncharacteristic show of frustration, barked at Walsh. "Why the hell did you wait six months before checking with Behan?"

Walsh had no answer.

Arnold Fraiman, who had since become a judge, acknowledged meeting with Serpico and Durk, and then sitting on the information. He said he thought it would be impossible to prove that an entire plainclothes unit was corrupt.

Michael Armstrong interrupted him. "I find it hard to understand why this important and serious allegation was not referred to someone."

"I normally would have done so," Fraiman said. "But he [Serpico] did not want to be identified."

"It is difficult to understand why this information was just dropped."

Chairman Knapp then asked Fraiman if it was possible that he'd committed an error in judgment.

"If I did so," Fraiman said, as though offering a valid explanation, "it was not the only error in my three years in the Department of Investigation."

Jay Kriegel started out by taking a similar approach to those before him. Kriegel confirmed that he'd met with Frank and Durk, and said he had passed the information on to his superiors—in this case, Mayor Lindsay. Initially, Kriegel said that Lindsay didn't want to go forward if the mayor had to hide the source of the information. Later, Kriegel reversed course entirely, saying Lindsay never knew of the allegations.

By the time the commission wrapped up its hearings, the pieces seemed easy to put together: Frank was an honest cop who'd tried to do something about a corrupt system, and nobody had listened.

In the days following the hearings, the case of Frank Serpico became national news:

> *The New York Times*: Serpico a 'Live Grenade' to Top
> Officers
> *The Philadelphia Inquirer*: N.Y. Cop Says He Was Warned
> During Probe
> *The Chicago Tribune*: Lindsay Aides Ignored Evidence of
> Police Graft, N.Y. Cop Says
> *The Los Angeles Times*: Ex-N.Y. Police Head Testifies on
> Corruption

Frank always felt that an independent body should monitor the police department, but he'd never longed for the spotlight. Like it or not, he now had both. He spent the winter of 1971 on sick leave, recuperating from his physical wounds and trying to resolve his emotional ones.

At thirty-six years old, he was questioning what to do with his life. He knew one thing: He was done being a cop. In June 1972, he submitted his resignation and, when the day came, went to police headquarters to pick up his last paycheck.

On Frank's way out the door, a cop asked him what he was going to do with his life now that he was no longer one of them.

Frank didn't have to think before answering.

"I'm going to live."

– A Final Word –

When I look back on the whole thing, I think the Knapp Commission called for what has always been needed in policing: outside accountability. A lot of officers were prosecuted and many lost their jobs. But reform didn't last. It never does.

One day I was being interviewed on a radio show and a cop called the station. He said that the day I testified was the darkest day for every cop in New York City. He said he was ashamed to go home and face his wife and children.

I said, "Why, what did you do wrong?"

He said, "Nothing."

So I asked him why he didn't support me. And do you know what he shouted at me without even thinking about it?

"What, and be an outcast like you?"

It's that kind of thinking that keeps the blue wall of silence alive today. And whistleblowers—or, as I like to call them, lamplighters, after Paul Revere—are just what that cop said we were: outcasts. When we try to bring injustice to light, we're told by government officials, "We can't afford a scandal; it would undermine public confidence in our police."

But the people who are part of that blue wall, the ones who are fighting to keep it standing, have missed the point.

That confidence is already broken.

Frank's Ideas

Frank suggests police departments create an environment in which honest cops are encouraged to speak up. To that end, he offers the following recommendations:

1. Strengthen the selection process for police recruits.
2. Provide ongoing training and simulations; show police officers how they're expected to behave and react.
3. Require police officers to be involved in the communities they serve.
4. Enforce the laws against everyone, including police officers. When cops do wrong, use them as examples of what not to do—that way, others know that this behavior won't be tolerated.
5. Support the good guys. Honest cops should be honored, promoted, and held up as positive role models.
6. Create and fund independent boards to review incidents of police corruption and brutality.

Epilogue

COMMISSIONER MURPHY INTRODUCED REFORM MEASURES, removed top officials, demoted inspectors, and planted insiders in station houses to uncover corruption within the ranks. In all, 1,134 officers were found guilty of corruption, and 59 were fired. In the 13th Division in Brooklyn—where Frank had been handed the envelope from Jewish Max—twenty-four plainclothes cops were indicted for taking a quarter of a million dollars a year from gambling bosses. Nineteen officers were convicted and fired.

In December 1972, after two and a half years of digging, the Knapp Commission delivered its final report. In the commission's words, during the time of its investigation "police corruption was found to be an extensive Department-wide phenomenon indulged in to some degree by a sizable majority of those on the force." The commission went on to say that organized crime was the "single biggest source of police corruption."

After testifying, Frank wanted to get as far away from New York as possible. Upon receiving his disability pension, the result of being shot on duty, he boarded a ship to Europe, taking his sheepdog, Alfie, with him.

While Frank was thousands of miles away, he became even more famous. In 1973, Viking Press published the book *Serpico* by journalist Peter Maas. It would sell three million copies. That same year, Paramount Pictures released a movie with the same name, putting

Frank's ordeal on the silver screen. The Academy of Motion Picture Arts and Sciences nominated Al Pacino for best actor in a leading role. In the words of *New Yorker* film critic Pauline Kael, Frank's story combined "Judas and Jesus in one small, wiry figure."

While in Europe, Frank married a Dutch woman who had two children. The four settled on a farm in the Netherlands, but after she died of cancer, and the children went to live with their maternal grandparents, Frank returned to the United States.

He continued to be ostracized by the NYPD. In the late '90s, when New York City opened a police museum, Frank offered his uniform and service revolver for display, only to have them rejected. It wasn't until 2022 that Mayor Eric Adams, a former police captain, made sure Frank was sent his proper medal of honor.

Frank now lives a private, comfortable life in upstate New York, a few hours north of the city he once patrolled. He built a one-room cabin in the woods. He grows his own food, raises chickens, and enriches his mind with music, books, and art.

The locals call him Paco.

Acknowledgments

When we suggested a book about Frank Serpico, our agent Jennifer Weltz championed the idea. Our editor Emily Feinberg helped us immeasurably by offering her support—along with her insights and a sharp red pen. We thank them both.

That said, the story is not ours; it belongs to Frank Serpico. He was and still is a hero, a dedicated cop with the crazy notion to stand up for what's right. His is a story that young people need to know, and he generously helped us tell it. Thank you, Paco.

Finally, we extend a sincere thanks to all police officers who do their jobs with honesty and integrity. We know you're there.

Glossary

10-10: Radio command meaning possible crime in progress, shots fired.

10-13: Radio command meaning officer in trouble, needs assistance.

APB: Short for "all-points bulletin." A radio message sent out to alert police officers to be on the lookout for someone or something in connection with a crime.

beat: The area patrolled by a police officer. A cop assigned to a beat is meant to develop a relationship with the community.

blue wall: Also known as "blue wall of silence." The unwritten code among police officers to remain silent when questioned about the conduct of their fellow officers.

brass: Also "top brass." High-ranking officials of a police department.

collar: An arrest.

CI: A "confidential informant" is someone who secretly gives information to the police about criminal activities. CIs are typically facing their own criminal charges. In exchange for information, their charges are reduced or dismissed.

cooping: The practice of sleeping on duty, often in a patrol car or secret location.

graft: A form of corruption in which a public official uses their authority in exchange for money or personal gain.

grand jury: A panel of sixteen to twenty-four people that decides whether there's enough evidence to bring a criminal charge against a suspect.

indictment: A formal notice made by a grand jury indicating there is enough evidence to put a suspect on trial.

numbers game: Also "numbers racket" or "policy game." A form of illegal gambling popular in low-income neighborhoods.

on the arm: Free, no charge.

pad: Also "the take" or "the nut." A system of corruption in which police officers receive bribes on a regular basis.

patronage: The practice of paying the boss to get promoted.

perpetrator: Also "perp." A person suspected by the police of committing a crime.

policy shop: A place where gamblers bet on numbers.

policy slip: Also "betting slip." A piece of paper showing the number bet by a gambler.

racketeering: Making money through a criminal operation.

riot detail: A police assignment to guard against riots.

shakedown: Also "shaking down." Bullying a person for money.

shoo-fly: A police officer who investigates other cops suspected of wrongdoing.

wearing a wire: Hiding an electronic recording device on your person to gather evidence against someone.

wop: An offensive term for a person of Italian birth or descent.

Source Notes

When compiling information for this book, we relied heavily on our interviews with Frank Serpico. We also leaned on newspaper accounts of the day, the book *Serpico* by Peter Maas, and the Baltimore Post-Examiner's nine-part series "Serpico Sets the Record Straight."

All of Frank's current-day recollections, which serve as interstitials between chapters, are taken from our interviews with him.

The following are sources we used in addition to this material.

PREFACE

The shooting at 778 Driggs Avenue has been well documented in many places, most notably, the Maas book. Other details are found in the Baltimore Post-Examiner series.

CHAPTER ONE

Information on the radio show *Gang Busters* can be found in O'Dell's "Gang Busters" essay at the Library of Congress. Episodes can be heard at the Internet Archive.

The passage on Fiorello La Guardia was taken largely from "La Guardia Regime Sets Precedents" in the *New York Times* and Graff's "Kind of Mayor La Guardia Was" in the *New York Times Magazine*. La Guardia's radio talk on July 8, 1945, can be heard online at the New York City Department of Records website.

The stories about Frank's childhood came from our interviews.

The training of police recruits and the classroom discussion is re-created from the *New York Times Magazine*'s "Police in the Making" and articles by Benjamin, "Sociology Is Part of Police Course," and Buckley, "Recruits Are Different," both in the *New York Times*.

The sidebar about New York's war on gambling is from the following *New York Times* articles: "Kennedy Orders War on Gambling," "Kennedy Demotes 4," Passant's "Kennedy Decries Gambling Apathy," and Grutzner's "Crackdown Thins Ranks."

The swearing-in ceremony and Stephen Kennedy's remarks came from the *New York Times*, "Policewoman Is Tops."

Information regarding Bedford-Stuyvesant can be found in the *New York Times*, "Negro Populace Rises," and Hymowitz's "Bed-Stuy's (Unfinished) Revival" in *City Journal*.

Frank's conversation about free meals is from our interviews.

For information on "cooping," we relied on three Burnham articles in the *New York Times*, "'Cooping': An Old Custom," "Top Police Officers Meet," and "Some Policemen Are Sleeping."

Frank related the story of his delivering the baby in our interviews.

More information on the Bureau of Criminal Identification can be found in Federici and Crews's *Daily News* article, "Our Cops—Finest with the Mostest."

Frank's experiences at the BCI, the 70th Precinct, and in Greenwich Village are from our interviews and the Maas book.

The story of Frank's off-duty chase on his motorcycle is from our interviews.

The conversation in the parking lot regarding the envelope from Jewish Max is from our interviews and the Maas book.

CHAPTER TWO

The sidebar on Mayor Lindsay is based on Federici and Wilson's *Daily News* article, "Splinters Fly"; the Associated Press's "Lindsay Thrives on Work"; Finnegan's *New Yorker* article, "How Police Unions Fight Reform"; and the *Akron Beacon Journal–New York*

Herald Tribune's "Lindsay Pushes N.Y. Crime Fight." We also relied on Charles Morris's *Cost of Good Intentions*.

We found the information regarding Frank's interactions with David Durk in Arnold's "How 2 Policemen Decided," and McFadden's "David Durk, Serpico's Ally, Dies," both in the *New York Times*. We picked up additional details during our interviews with Frank. Durk's "help an old lady" and "shopkeeper" quotes are from his December 21, 1971, testimony before the Knapp Commission; we found them in the McFadden obituary. For more information on Frank and Durk's efforts, we suggest Daley's "Portrait of an Honest Cop" in *New York* magazine.

The section on the Department of Investigation, including Frank and Durk's meeting with Philip Foran and Frank's experience at the Nine-O, was found in the Maas book. Frank provided more details during our interviews. The same is true for the passage about the 7th Division, including the scene with Robert Stanard and Pasquale Trozzo at Otto's Bar and Grill.

The sidebar about the Harry Gross scandal is from Honig's "2 Needed to Carry," Freeman's "New York Police Purge," Perlmutter's "Monaghan Ousts 23," and McFadden's "Lonely Death," all in the *New York Times*, and Wiener and Patterson's "Gross Bookie Empire" in the *Daily News*.

CHAPTER THREE

The Maas book covers Frank's interactions with Carmello Zumatto. We added details from our interviews with Frank.

The sidebar about the roots of corruption is from Roosevelt's *Atlantic* article, "Municipal Administration"; the *Chicago Tribune*'s "Tell of Their Money"; and the *Brooklyn Daily Eagle*'s "Byrnes to Go." Roosevelt's letter to his sister can be found at the Theodore Roosevelt Digital Library.

Frank's interactions with Cornelius Behan, including his conversation by the Van Wyck Expressway, are from the Maas book and the Baltimore Post-Examiner's multipart series. Frank added more details during our interviews. Additional information on Behan, John Walsh, and Howard Leary can be found in Burnham's "Police Portrait" in the *New York Times*. The "shoo-fly" quote comes from the *Times*'s "Taciturn Detective."

CHAPTER FOUR

Frank's conversation with Stephen Killorin is a compilation of several meetings covered in the Maas book; Frank also supplied additional details during our interviews. The same is true for Frank's conversation with Jay Kriegel, and with Jules Sachson in Sachson's car.

The information regarding Frank and Sachson searching the bodega and arresting Dolores Carreras is from Burnham's "Bronx Gambler" in the *New York Times*.

The sidebar about the numbers racket is from Grutzner's "Dimes Make Millions" and Roth's "Gamblers Here Operate Numbers," both in the *New York Times*.

Frank's meeting with Burton Roberts, his appearance in front of the grand jury, and his altercation with a fellow officer in Manhattan North come from the Maas book and Frank's firsthand recollections shared during our interviews.

You can find the grand jury indictments of February 11, 1969, in the following sources: Renner and Swift's "8 Cops Indicted" in *Newsday*, O'Grady and Lee's "Cops Indicted" in the *Daily News*, and Collier's "8 City Policemen Arrested" in the *New York Times*.

The conversation between Frank and Delise in Delise's office, as well as the stories of their working in tandem, are from the Maas book and our interviews with Frank.

We pieced together Frank and Durk's meeting with David Burnham at the Greenwich Village coffee shop from our interviews with both Frank and Burnham.

The conversation between Frank and Delise in Delise's living room is from our interviews with Frank.

We constructed the meeting in the *New York Times* conference room with Frank, Durk, Delise, Burnham, and Arthur Gelb by combining several meetings from the Maas book, as well as our interviews with both Frank and Burnham.

CHAPTER FIVE

The scene with Frank in the back seat of the unmarked patrol car is from our interviews with Frank.

Burnham's front-page story, "Graft Paid to Police Here," can be found in the *New York Times* of April 25, 1970. Frank's reaction to the article came from our interviews with him.

Burnham's follow-up front-page stories on police corruption, "Gamblers' Links to Police" and "Police Corruption Fosters Distrust," ran in the *New York Times* on April 26 and April 27, 1970.

Howard Leary's comment about the *New York Times* being unfair can be found in Farrell's *New York Times* article, "Leary Assails Articles in Times."

Mayor Lindsay's quotes come from "Mayor Asks Aid," which ran right below Burnham's April 25 story on the *New York Times* front page.

Howard Leary's statement to the police precincts can be found in Illson's *New York Times* article "Leary Vows 'No Reprisals.'"

Frank and Burton Roberts's conversation before Frank's court appearance and his testimony on the witness stand are taken from recollections shared by Frank during our interviews. For the trial we also leaned on Burnham's *New York Times* articles "Bronx Gambler" and "Antigambling Unit" as well as two *Daily News* stories: "Testifies She Paid Off Cops" and "Convicted Cop."

The conversation in which Burton Roberts suggests that Howard Leary promote Frank is taken from the Maas book.

The part about Howard Leary's resignation is from Poster and Lee's "Holiday Bombshell" in the *Daily News*.

The conversation in which the sergeant tells Frank that big

money can be made in Brooklyn was pieced together from the Maas book and our interviews with Frank.

The sidebar about the Michael Dowd drug ring is from Treaster's "Officer Flaunted Corruption" and "Convicted Police Officer," both in the *New York Times*, and Gelman and Kocieniewski's "It's Called the Cop Casino" in *Newsday*.

CHAPTER SIX

The shooting at 778 Driggs Avenue, including the scenes outside the building and Frank's actions on the roof, is taken from the Maas book and our interviews with Frank. We also relied on Daley's "Portrait of an Honest Cop" in *New York* magazine and Kilgannon's online video, "Watching 'Serpico' with Serpico."

CHAPTER SEVEN

We pieced together Frank's stay at Greenpoint Hospital from the Maas book, our interviews with Frank, and Burnham's *New York Times* article "Mayor Visits." Mayor Lindsay's statement and the report of Frank's condition as "fair" are from the same sources.

The conversation in the hospital between Frank and Arthur Cesare comes from the Maas book and our interviews with Frank. The same is true for the anonymous "get well" card and Frank's return to his apartment on Perry Street.

The department's questioning of Gary Roteman and Arthur Cesare comes from the Maas book.

CHAPTER EIGHT

Frank's appearance in front of the Knapp Commission was widely covered at the time. We relied on Armstrong's *They Wished They Were Honest*, as well as the following newspaper accounts: Gelman's *Newsday* article, "'Meat-Eaters and Grass-Eaters'"; the *New York Times*'s "Excerpts from Testimony Before Knapp Commission," "Excerpts from the Testimony by Serpico," "Final Knapp Report," and "Report Says Police Corruption"; Arnold's *New York Times* articles "Serpico's Lonely Journey" and "Leary Asks Why"; and Federici and Meskil's *Daily News* articles "Hands Tied on Cop Graft" and "Knapp Probe Told."

Frank's prepared statement appears with the excerpts of his testimony in the *Times*.

The sidebar about modern-day whistleblowers is based on Barton, Duret, and Murphy's *USA Today* article, "Behind the Blue Wall"; Goodman's "Officer Who Disclosed Police Misconduct" in the *New York Times*; Broadwater's *Baltimore Sun* article, "Baltimore to Pay $42K"; and Gorner's "Chicago Cop Alleges Cover-Up" in the *Chicago Tribune*. Sergeant Lambert's "stand for something" quote comes from Solotaroff's "The Untouchables" in *Rolling Stone*. The sergeant's Serpico line is from Gorner's *Chicago Tribune* article.

The testimony of Behan, Walsh, Fraiman, and Kriegel before the Knapp Commission is taken from the Maas book. More on Walsh can be found in Burnham's "Walsh at Hearing"; more on Kriegel can be found in Burnham's "Kriegel Gets Aid," both of which are in the *New York Times*.

Frank's plans for life after the Knapp Commission, as well as his comment "I'm going to live," are from our interviews with Frank.

A FINAL WORD

The sidebar in which Frank offers his advice to modern-day police departments is from his online article at Politico, "Police Are Still Out of Control."

EPILOGUE

We found the numbers associated with Commissioner Murphy's reform measures in Buckley's "Murphy Among the 'Meat-Eaters,'" Kaplan's "24 Police Indicated," and Rabb's "Codd Dismisses," all of which ran in the *New York Times*.

The commission's quotes are pulled from the *Knapp Commission Report*.

Kael's review of *Serpico* appears in her *New Yorker* article, "The Hero as Freak."

Frank's marriage in Europe is from Kilgannon's "Serpico on Serpico" in the *New York Times*.

Frank's receiving his medal of honor certificate is covered in Annese's *Daily News* article, "Frank Serpico Finally Gets His Formal Medal of Honor."

Bibliography

BOOKS

Armstrong, Michael F. *They Wished They Were Honest: The Knapp Commission and New York City Police Corruption*. New York: Columbia University Press, 2012.

Commission to Investigate Allegations of Police Corruption and the City's Anti-Corruption Procedures. *The Knapp Commission Report on Police Corruption*. New York: Braziller, 1973.

Daley, Robert. *Target Blue: An Insider's View of the N.Y.P.D.* New York: Delacorte Press, 1973.

Maas, Peter. *Serpico*. New York: Viking, 1973.

Morris, Charles R. *The Cost of Good Intentions: New York City and the Liberal Experiment, 1960–1975*. New York: Norton, 1980.

MAGAZINES

Bekiempis, Victoria. "Still Chasing Serpico." *Newsweek*, December 5, 2013.

Cook, Fred J. "The Pusher-Cop: The Institutionalizing of Police Corruption." *New York*, August 16, 1971.

Daley, Robert. "Portrait of an Honest Cop: Target for Attack." *New York*, May 3, 1971.

Finnegan, William. "How Police Unions Fight Reform." *New Yorker*, July 27, 2020.

Hirsh, Michael. "Serpico on Police Racism: 'We Have This Virus Among Us.'" *Foreign Policy*, June 11, 2020.

Hymowitz, Kay S. "Bed-Stuy's (Unfinished) Revival." *City Journal*,

Summer 2013. city-journal.org/html/bed-stuy's-unfinished
-revival-13581.html.

Johnson, Roberta Ann. "Whistleblowing and the Police."
Rutgers University Journal of Law and Urban Policy 3, no. 1
(November 20, 2005): 74–83.

Kael, Pauline. "The Hero as Freak." *New Yorker*, December 17, 1973.

Lepore, Jill. "The Invention of the Police: Why Did American
Policing Get So Big, So Fast? The Answer, Mainly, Is Slavery."
New Yorker, July 13, 2020.

Roosevelt, Theodore. "Municipal Administration: The New York
Police Force." *Atlantic*, September 1897.

Shaer, Matthew. "134 Minutes with Frank Serpico." *New York*,
September 27, 2013.

Solotaroff, Paul. "The Untouchables: An Investigation into the
Violence of the Chicago Police." *Rolling Stone*, November 19,
2020.

Time. "CRIME: Listen to the Mocking Bird." May 19, 1952.

NEWSPAPERS

Akron Beacon Journal–New York Herald Tribune. "Lindsay Pushes
N.Y. Crime Fight." *Akron Beacon Journal.* October 1, 1965.

Annese, John. "Frank Serpico Finally Gets His Formal Medal of
Honor." *Daily News* (New York), February 4, 2022.

Arnold, Martin. "Crusading Policeman: Francisco [sic] Vincent
Serpico." *New York Times*, May 11, 1971.

———. "How 2 Policemen Decided to Fight Graft." *New York
Times*, June 20, 1970.

———. "Leary Asks Why He Wasn't Told of Police Corruption in
the Bronx Early Enough." *New York Times*, December 21, 1971.

———. "Serpico a 'Live Grenade' to Top Officers." *New York
Times*, December 17, 1971.

———. "Serpico's Lonely Journey to Knapp Witness Stand."
New York Times, December 15, 1971.

Associated Press. "Lindsay Thrives on Work." *Ithaca Journal*, November 3, 1965.

Barton, Gina, Daphne Duret, and Brett Murphy. "Behind the Blue Wall of Silence." *USA Today*, December 9, 2021.

Benjamin, Philip. "Sociology Is Part of Police Course." *New York Times*, February 28, 1959.

Broadwater, Luke. "Baltimore to Pay $42K to Whistle-Blower Former Officer Who Found Rat on Car." *Baltimore Sun*, June 1, 2016.

Brooklyn Daily Eagle. "Byrnes to Go." December 30, 1894.

Buckley, Tom. "Murphy Among the 'Meat-Eaters.'" *New York Times Magazine*, December 19, 1971.

———. "The Recruits Are Different and So Is Police Academy." *New York Times*, July 6, 1973.

Burnham, David. "Antigambling Unit Is Termed Corrupt at Policeman's Trial." *New York Times*, June 18, 1970.

———. "Bronx Gambler Tells of Monthly Payoffs to Police." *New York Times*, June 24, 1970.

———. "'Cooping': An Old Custom Under Fire." *New York Times*, December 22, 1968.

———. "15 Police Trials Begin Tomorrow." *New York Times*, May 2, 1971.

———. "Gamblers' Links to Police Lead to Virtual 'Licensing.'" *New York Times*, April 26, 1970.

———. "Graft Paid to Police Here Said to Run Into Millions." *New York Times*, April 25, 1970.

———. "Knapp Panel Says Walsh and Others Ignored Tips by U.S. on Police Crimes." *New York Times*, December 28, 1972.

———. "Knapp Says Laws Spur Police Graft." *New York Times*, June 7, 1970.

———. "Kriegel Gets Aid on Lindsay Book." *New York Times*, February 24, 1974.

———. "Lindsay Appoints Corruption Unit." *New York Times,* May 22, 1970.

———. "The Mayor Visits 'a Very Brave Man.'" *New York Times,* February 5, 1971.

———. "Paper on Cooping Gets a High Grade." *New York Times,* August 3, 1969.

———. "Perjury Laid to Police Captain in Denial of Serpico Testimony." *New York Times,* April 6, 1972.

———. "Police Corruption Fosters Distrust in the Ranks Here." *New York Times,* April 27, 1970.

———. "Police Establish Corruption Curbs Under New Units." *New York Times,* August 27, 1970.

———. "A Police Portrait: Leary and His Five Closest Associates." *New York Times,* November 10, 1969.

———. "Prosecutor Called to the Stand in Policeman's Trial in Bronx." *New York Times,* June 20, 1970.

———. "Serpico Tells of Delay on Police Inquiry." *New York Times,* December 15, 1971.

———. "Some Policemen Are Found to Be Sleeping on Duty." *New York Times,* December 16, 1968.

———. "Top Police Officers Meet Today to Discuss Sleeping Patrolmen." *New York Times,* December 17, 1968.

———. "Walsh at Hearing: Forgot Graft Report." *New York Times,* December 17, 1971.

Chicago Tribune. "Tell of Their Money." December 30, 1894.

Collier, Barnard L. "8 City Policemen Arrested in Inquiry on Numbers Games." *New York Times,* February 12, 1969.

Daily News (New York). "Convicted Cop Faces 7 Years for Perjury," July 2, 1970.

———. "Testifies She Paid Off Cops," June 24, 1970.

Farrell, William E. "Leary Assails Articles in Times on Police Corruption as 'Unfair.'" *New York Times,* April 29, 1970.

Federici, William, and Watson Crews Jr. "Our Cops—Finest with the Mostest." *Daily News* (New York), December 1, 1963.

Federici, William, and Paul Meskil. "Cop Says He Was Warned to Keep Quiet About Graft." *Daily News* (New York), December 15, 1971.

———. "Hands Tied on Cop Graft: Lindsay Aide." *Daily News* (New York), December 21, 1971.

———. "Knapp Probe Told of 9-Month Stall." *Daily News* (New York), December 16. 1971.

———, and Sidney Kline. "Cops Parlay New Ways to Eliminate Bookies." *New York Daily News*, April 29, 1962.

Federici, William, and Harry Schlegel. "Review Board's Innovations to Stay." *Daily News* (New York), November 11, 1966.

Federici, William, and Theo Wilson. "The Splinters Fly from Many Sides on Review Board." *Daily News* (New York), June 11, 1965.

Freeman, Ira Henry. "New York Police Purge Winding Up Gross Case." *New York Times*, September 7, 1952.

Gelman, David. "'Meat-Eaters and Grass-Eaters.'" *Newsday*, August 14, 1972.

Gelman, Mitch, and David Kocieniewski. "It's Called the Cop Casino." *Newsday*, May 21, 1992.

Goldman, John J. "Ex-N.Y. Police Head Testifies on Corruption." *Los Angeles Times*, December 21, 1971.

Goodman, J. David. "Officer Who Disclosed Police Misconduct Settles Suit." *New York Times*, September 29, 2015.

Gorner, Jeremy. "Chicago Cop Alleges Cover-Up in Police Shooting: 'I'm Going to Feel like Serpico, Basically.'" *Chicago Tribune*, March 5, 2019.

Graff, Henry F. "The Kind of Mayor La Guardia Was." *New York Times Magazine*, October 22, 1961.

Grutzner, Charles. "Crackdown Thins Ranks of Bookies." *New York Times*, October 1, 1963.

———. "Dimes Make Millions for Numbers Racket." *New York Times*, June 26, 1964.

Honig, Milton. "2 Needed to Carry Gross 'Ice' Money." *New York Times*, January 23, 1951.

Illson, Murray. "Leary Vows 'No Reprisals' to Police Telling of Graft." *New York Times*, May 17, 1970.

Johnston, Richard J. H. "86 Are Indicted in Bookie Inquiry." *New York Times*, April 29, 1965.

Kaplan, Morris. "24 Police Indicted in a Bribery Case." *New York Times*, May 3, 1972.

Kilgannon, Corey. "Serpico on Serpico." *New York Times*, January 22, 2010.

Kirkman, Edward. "A Shoot-the-Works War Is Declared on Gamblers." *Daily News* (New York), April 19, 1961.

McFadden, Robert D. "David Durk, Serpico's Ally Against Graft, Dies at 77." *New York Times*, November 13, 2012.

———. "The Lonely Death of a Man Who Made a Scandal." *New York Times*, April 5, 1986.

McNamara, Joseph. "Mayor Socks Critics of His Fight on Crime." *Daily News* (New York), May 17, 1965.

McShane, Larry. "No Quit in Famed NYPD Whistleblower." *Daily News* (New York), December 23, 2012.

Mustain, Gene. "Brothers in Blue: Frank Serpico." Big Town Biography. *Daily News* (New York), June 1, 1999.

New York Times. "Excerpts from Testimony Before Knapp Commission." December 21, 1971.

———. "Excerpts from the Testimony by Serpico." December 15, 1971.

———. "Final Knapp Report." Editorial. January 13, 1973.

———. "Kennedy Demotes 4 Police Officers in Gambling Cases." February 13, 1959.

———. "Kennedy Orders War on Gambling." February 24, 1959.

———. "La Guardia Regime Sets Precedents." May 7, 1945.

———. "Mayor Asks Aid from All in Inquiry on Corruption." April 25, 1970.

———. "Negro Populace Rises in Bedford-Stuyvesant." August 12, 1963.

———. "Policewoman Is Tops." April 12, 1960.

———. "Report Says Police Corruption in 1971 Involved Well over Half on the Force." December 28, 1972.

———. "Taciturn Detective: John Francis Walsh." January 21, 1961.

New York Times Magazine. "Police in the Making." May 15, 1960.

O'Grady, Daniel, and Henry Lee. "Cops Indicted on Tie to Cosa Policy Ring." *Daily News* (New York), February 12, 1969.

Passant, Guy. "Kennedy Decries Gambling Apathy." *New York Times*, March 1, 1960.

Perlmutter, Emanuel. "Major Crime Up 52% in Subways, 9% Citywide." *New York Times*, February 10, 1965.

———. "Monaghan Ousts 23 Accused by Gross; 6 Men Are Cleared." *New York Times*, February 25, 1953.

Pittsburgh Courier. "New York Has New Police Review Board." Editorial. July 23, 1966.

Poster, Thomas, and Henry Lee. "A Holiday Bombshell: Leary to Quit." *Daily News* (New York), September 6, 1970.

Powledge, Fred. "Pick a Number from 000 to 999." *New York Times*, December 6, 1964.

Raab, Selwyn. "Codd Dismisses 19 Former Plainclothes Police Officers in a Bribery Scandal." *New York Times*, November 19, 1974.

———. "Similarities in Inquiries into Crimes by Officers." *New York Times*, October 3, 1993.

Renner, Tom, and Maurice Swift. "8 Cops Indicted in NY Policy Probe." *Newsday*, February 12, 1969.

Roth, Jack. "Gamblers Here Operate Numbers Game in Open." *New York Times*, May 7, 1967.

Star, Cima. "Brave and Honest Cop." *Daily Courier* (Connellsville, PA), July 21, 1971.

Tolchin, Martin. "Bedford-Stuyvesant Residents to Fight Crime with Police Dogs." *New York Times*, April 2, 1965.

Treaster, Joseph B. "Convicted Police Officer Receives a Sentence of at Least 11 Years." *New York Times*, July 12, 1994.

———. "Officer Flaunted Corruption, and His Superiors Ignored It." *New York Times*, July 7, 1994.

United Press International. "N.Y. Cop Says He Was Warned During Probe." *Philadelphia Inquirer*, December 15, 1971.

Wiener, Ernest, and Neal Patterson. "Gross Bookie Empire Outlined to Cop Jury." *Daily News* (New York), September 18, 1951.

Zullo, Joseph. "Lindsay Aides Ignored Evidence of Police Graft, N.Y. Cop Says." *Chicago Tribune*, December 15, 1971.

ONLINE RESOURCES

Internet Archive. "Gang Busters—88 Episodes of the Old Time Radio Crime Drama." archive.org/details/gang-busters -1955–04–02–885-the-case-of-the-mistreated-lady.

Kilgannon, Corey. "Watching 'Serpico' with Serpico." Photography by Librado Romero. *New York Times*, January 22, 2010. Video, 4:27. nytimes.com/video/nyregion/1247466675385/watching -serpico-with-serpico.html.

La Guardia, Fiorello. "Talk to the People," July 8, 1945. WNYC Radio. New York City Department of Records and Information Services. Audio recording. nycma.lunaimaging .com/luna/servlet/detail/RECORDSPHOTOUNITARC-26- 26-1339456-135185.

O'Dell, Cary. "Gang Busters." Library of Congress, 2008. loc
	.gov/static/programs/national-recording-preservation-board
	/documents/GangBusters.pdf.

Poppa, Doug. "Serpico Sets the Record Straight." Baltimore
	Post-Examiner. Nine parts, July 15–August 9, 2017.
	baltimorepostexaminer.com/category/news/special-reports
	/serpico-sets-the-record-straight.

Roosevelt, Theodore. Letter to Anna Roosevelt, May 18, 1895.
	Theodore Roosevelt Collection. MS Am 1834 (454). Harvard
	College Library. Theodore Roosevelt Digital Library.
	Dickinson State University. theodorerooseveltcenter.org
	/Research/Digital-Library/Record?libID=o283606.

Serpico, Frank. "The Police Are Still Out of Control; I Should
	Know." Politico, October 23, 2014. www.politico.com
	/magazine/story/2014/10/the-police-are-still-out-of-control
	-112160/.

INTERVIEWS

Burnham, David: February 4, 2021.

Serpico, Frank: February 18, 2021; February 19, 2021; March 17, 2021;
	May 22, 2021; September 21, 2021; April 26, 2022; October 22,
	2022.

Image Credits

Index

Note: Page references in *italics* indicate photographs or illustrations.

disability from shooting, 2, 96,
110
help from apartment tenant,
91, 97
hospital and recovery, 93–95
hospital visit from Cesare, 95
hospital visit from Murphy and
Lindsay, 94
last rites administered, 92
left by partners to die, 91, 94, 96
Mambo as shooter, 90–91
possibility of shooting as set
up, 98
Sims, Brook, 41–42
Stanard, Robert
bribes taken by, 36–38, 51
corruption case against, 61–62,
64, 71
guilty of perjury to grand jury, 80
protection money paid to, 58
sense of entitlement, 42–43
tagged as corrupt by Frank, 55
testimony to grand jury, 62
tough guy persona of, 35
on trial in Bronx Supreme
Court for perjury, 79–80
Strong, William, 44, 45

T
take. *See* pad
13th Division, 24, 109
Trozzo, Pasquale, 36–37, 42

U
undercover work, 49, 50, 64
USA Today on police
whistleblowers (2021), 103

V
Vanderbilt, Cornelius, 45
vice duty at 18th Precinct, 63–64

W
Wagner, Robert, 27
Walsh, John, *47*
failure to respond to corruption
reports, 69
Frank going to newspapers as
way to motivate, 67
Knapp Commission
questioning of, 104
reputation for cleaning up
NYPD, 47–48, 104
Roberts's interest in Walsh's
failure to deal with
corruption, 61
whistleblowers
Frank becoming outcast as,
2–3, 32–33, 65, 104, 107,
110
laws to protect, 103
police hatred of, 50, 103–104

Z
Zumatto, Carmello
arrest made for show by,
41–42
case against, 61, 64, 71,
79–80
on Frank's list of crooked cops,
55
protection money paid to,
58
share of the pad offered to
Frank by, 40